DWARKAMAI

A Magical Trip

DWARKAMAI

A Magical Trip

SUJAY KHANDELWAL

STERLING PUBLISHERS (P) LTD.
Regd. Office: A1/256 Safdarjung Enclave, New Delhi-110029.
Cin: U22110DL1964PTC211907
Phone: +91 82877 98380/ +91 120-6251823
e-mail: mail@sterlingpublishers.in
www.sterlingpublishers.in

Dwarkamai: A Magical Trip
© 2022 Sujay Khandelwal
ISBN 978 93 93853 04 2

All rights are reserved.
No part of this publication may be reproduced, stored in a retrieval system or transmitted, in any form or by any means, mechanical, photocopying, recording or otherwise, without prior written permission of the original publisher.

Printed in India

Printed and Published by Sterling Publishers Pvt. Ltd., Plot No. 13, Ecotech-III, Greater Noida - 201306, Uttar Pradesh, India

Contents

	Foreword	7
	Introduction	9
1.	The Calling	15
2.	The Journey	19
3.	Touchdown – Mumbai, Destination – Shirdi	23
4.	Change, Unchanged	27
5.	Darshan – Finally	31
6.	Just My Luck(S)	37
7.	The Divine & His Miracles	43
8.	The Miracle Morning	51
9.	Sai, I Am Here	57
10.	Tears Of Divine Love	63
11.	Showers Of Blessings	67
12.	From Connect To Consciousness	71
13.	Grace Overflowing	75
14.	The Magic Continues	79
15.	Beginning, All Over Again	87

FOREWORD

Sujay and I are first cousins and I have known him since his childhood. We had our first spiritual experience together when we went for a spiritual retreat to Bangalore in October 2019 and I was so delighted to see how much at home Sujay felt in that environment.

When Sujay asked me to write the foreword for this book, my heart leapt with joy. It was so gratifying for me to see someone from my own family, to make an effort to bring spiritual awareness in the world. Spirituality comes in many flavours - devotion, prayer, chanting, practices, serving people. As a practicing spiritualist for over 15 years (and being a meditation teacher), I have realized that our lives are a mix of highs and lows, sorrow and joys; though it is always up to us whether we make it joyous or painful. Sujay has opted to look at the brighter side of life and make it work not only to uplift himself but to take up the cause of rehabilitation of alcoholics and brighten up their lives too.

It's so heartwarming to see such a deep book of Sai's love and grace in a devotee's life. It's a beautiful story of Sujay's trip to the holy site of Shirdi and the magical moments of his experiences there. It's wonderful how Sujay despite having such a busy life, could carve out time for his trip to Shirdi (out of his intense longing for Sai darshan) and how Sai showered him with His love and presence in so many ways. This book is a perfect depiction that if you take one step towards the Divine, He will take ten steps towards you, as happened during Sujay's trip to Shirdi.

Chavi Kejriwal

INTRODUCTION

Everyone goes through ups and downs in life.

The worst period of my life was when I was in utter despair, but it was also the transformation period of my life. It was 1 phase which ultimately made me go deep down to introspect and realize true value of the biggest gift from Sai: Human Life. Love, tolerance, patience and acceptance are the key towards serenity, I realized this though my process of transformation. I had lived my entire life for my own self, on the motives that served just me. I was self-centered and selfish, but now it's my time to give back to the society. When I recognized this, I found the purpose of my life: to be in service, to be available for others, to think of others, to bring a few smiles on the faces of others.

A few months before the onset of the pandemic, I got myself registered and certified as a volunteer in an NGO in the name of Hope Foundation in Kolkata. I had just begun service when, in less than 2months time, the pandemic began to spread. Instead of staying back at home to remain protected, I chose to go to the Girls' home to arrange ration for them. Fear had gripped the nation. People were scared, even to help.

For nearly a week, I went to different places daily to arrange the ration. Ultimately, it was arranged for 3 months. I could do it myself without thinking twice but I raised funds from the society so that all could get connected to this social cause. That was the actual beginning of my service towards putting others before my own self.

Great journeys start with small steps, they say. I understood the meaning of this when I got the opportunity to start with this NGO by the name of Sabhuri Rehabilitation Centre under the Shiv Chandra Charitable trust. The trust itself gets its name from my father's name, Late Shri Shiv Shanker Khandelwal and my mother's name Smt. Chandra Prabha Khandelwal. What started off as my dream is today a mission that the whole Khandelwal family is committed to.

My eldest brother, Ajay, has been the most important person in this journey. He is the one who has never lost hope in me. While all, including myself, had lost hope in me, he was the one who believed that, times would change for the good. Ajay Bhaiya is 13 years older than me. Needless to say, he is more of a father figure to me. But in these times of despair, he stood by me more as a friend. The moments of despair brought in lots of pain which had once become unbearable. I have hurt many people through my words or my actions, may be indirectly, or may be sometimes, directly. As I look back at those times, my heart fills with the highest form of gratitude to all of them who have always stood by me. They kept me alive to reach this stage in life when I do not need any external stuff to bring happiness inside me. The second innings of my life has just begun, which is nothing but a blessing of Mere Sai.

Sai has been there in my life after my marriage. My Wife, Riya is a devotee of Sai since her childhood. She is the one behind my connection with Sai Baba.

Sai is one whose existence and presence is defined by You. If you believe in Him, He is everything and if you do not, then He is nothing. For some he is a Fakir, for few He is a Guru, for others, He is a friend, a pal or even a parent. Like a father, he has saved me many a times from just slipping away from Him, always carrying me in His arms and protecting me. Like a mother he has loved and cared for me. I can talk to Him like a friend, about anything and everything now. Like a pal, I remain so casual with him always that I often call him buddha (old man). Like a fakir he teaches me the value of humanity over money. Like a Guru he always shows me the direction of my life, always directing me towards my Goals in life, to be in service.

I remember a certain moment of utter despair in my life when once, in my drunken state, I had bashed one of the three beautiful pictures of Sai which are placed at a prominent place in my house. That blow was so hard that it had brought that picture of Sai down on the floor with a big sound. It was quite late in the night when the sound echoed in the house, breaking through walls and windows. The next moment, Riya came running out of the bedroom to check what had happened. I was crying at that moment. I was resentful towards Baba for making me so dependent on alcohol. I thought that he had made me into a bad person, who couldn't quit drinking and was finishing up everything in life. My Love, my family, my relationship, my social status, my health, my money, everything was bleeding. I wanted to quit but my mental obsession didn't let me do it at that time. My own will power was failing me too, even though I believed that I was a strong enough person, an achiever in life. This used to give me a sense of defeat. I began to tag myself with a label of a loser, just like others did to me.

It was Riya who has seen my despair and my state of utter hopelessness. Her shoulders have not only given me strength and support, but had become absolutely wet with the tears which I used to shed each day. My heart used to cry each moment, but my eyes would shed tears on a few instances only. Even though I felt my weaknesses, I didn't want to portray it ever. But somehow, I couldn't resist it either. It had become a part of my life. I would drink to relieve myself from the guilt and the pain and then get more pain by drinking again. Those momentary reliefs followed by increased pain created a vicious cycle in my life. Today, I am able to laugh at my weaknesses when I think about those times, but at that time, it was taking a toll on me.

Sai has always showered his unconditional love in my life. Sai has helped me, He kept me alive till now to see the change and has given me a new purpose of life. My deepest gratitude to Him for the blessings I feel each moment and the miracles which are now a part of my life.

25th of February, the release date of this book, is a very significant day for me. This book is being completed at the right time. This day is the Birthday of my Love, my wife, Riya. She's one of the biggest gifts of Sai in my life. Had she not been there in my life, I couldn't have ever been able to connect to Sai. She is my inspiration who has always told me one sentence throughout my life.

"Sujay, you have immense potential in you and you are just wasting away your life by not living up to your potential."

Her words keep inspiring me each moment towards uplifting myself towards my growth as a human. These almost two years of sobriety has also been difficult and wasn't easy enough in the beginning, but now with the faith and the gratitude which have grown roots inside me, I have no fears of relapse.

Riya is a graceful and beautiful lady who has faith and wisdom as her core strengths. Humility and Love are her forces. Her understanding nature and knowledge in all subjects of life, compliment her nature perfectly, making her an interesting company to be with. A Dog lover, a genuine human, she carries values of life to bring about smiles on so many faces.

Another significance of this date is the birthday of the editor of this book, Amrita Nilesh. She is another devotee of Sai who has put life to this story. She has relived the moments with me while we edited this story. Blessings of Sai that one fine day I abruptly called her to share a blog that I had written and wished her to read it. Little did I realize at that time that what I had written was almost a book. When she brought that to my notice, it kindled my desire to publish my book. She gave me so much of ideas over the first phone call that there was looking back from there on. She is a strong lady, a self-made business woman who has lived life on her terms and upgraded herself to be a prominent coach and trainer, blogger, writer, editor, social worker, an ardent animal lover and above all, a patriot. Words aren't enough alone to describe her.

My deepest gratitude to her for working on this book with me. It's a blessing of Sai and His desire that this book be published.

1

THE CALLING

I turned my wrist to take a look at my watch. My neck hurt as I tried to see the time, possibly because of the bad posture in which I had fallen asleep. Seated in my aisle seat numbered 23F, I could hear the low humming sound of the aircraft. The cool breeze from the tiny fan above pierced through my white Hilfiger jacket and made me shiver. I was in an early morning Air Asia flight from Kolkata to Mumbai. This 0530 am flight was the only suitable one I could find for my much-awaited trip. There are many flights from Kolkata to Mumbai, but I was headed to Shirdi and given my limited time, my choices became far more limited. Shirdi airport was not operating at that time for any direct flights, so the best suitable option was via Mumbai.

I had been waiting for this trip since Durga Puja. Flights had started operating as the lockdown fizzled out, but Sai Mandir was still closed. I was getting restless, I wanted to meet my Sai. I knew He hears me, feels me. I believed that my calling would come.

Finally, I received two messages from Sai, one via Rishi, my nephew and another one through Prita, my sister-in-law. They both had visited the mandir the previous week post lockdown and vouched for the fantastic arrangements there in view of the pandemic. As I heard about their visits, my mind silently pleaded to Sai, "Baba, when will I be able to come to see you at Shirdi?"

It's known commonly that none can visit Shirdi unless Baba calls them. This was proven again when Rishi managed to visit the temple twice while he was in Shirdi, whereas his wife, Surbhi, couldn't visit Baba in spite of being in Shirdi for three days. "Baba's wish, whom he calls", we knew it.

I kept talking to Sai in my mind, "So many projects are running together, even the Big Bang celebration party is due next week. How will I be able to come now, Baba?" My heart was restless to go to Shirdi, but the logical brain said otherwise. "No, you can't go now", the brain screamed, but my heart raced at the thought of meeting Sai.

I silenced my head and got to work, forgetting about the trip. The day went on as usual. But, that evening, as I watched my favourite show "Mere Sai" on SonyLiv app, a thought came to my mind. "Baba is calling you over to seek His blessings. That's why He has sent messages through two people." Suddenly I felt my heart thumping in my chest with an indomitable desire to meet Sai. But the brain was still not pleased. It asked me to get over the 'stupid idea'.

I had been working for almost 12hrs a day without any breaks for some time now. I was trying to meet up to my own level of expectations from myself for completion of my projects. I was working on five different projects simultaneously. "You have no time for a trip now", I said to myself, shattering my own heart. It's not easy to sleep with a heartbreak, but I tried. Next morning, I woke up earlier than usual.

After completing my morning routine and my meditation, I texted my travel agent almost on an impulse. I wanted to check if there were any chopper services available from Mumbai to Shirdi, so that I could complete the trip faster. The reply came later in the day in two alphabets: NO.

The reply wasn't a surprise, but it wasn't a disappointment either, because I had found a way out by then. "If I complete the targeted work by Friday, I can take a break on Saturday and return back on Sunday", I said to myself and that was it. Finally, my mind was made.

Not a moment more was wasted. My tickets were booked.

"I am going to meet my Sai. Yippee!", my heart could barely hold the joy. That night, I couldn't sleep until 0130hrs, such was my level of excitement. I started visualizing myself there in front of Baba. My last visit to Shirdi was more than three years ago with Riya, my wife. Currently, she is unavailable to join me there. All my previous visits to Shirdi were invariably with her, except for two instances: once when I was there with my cousin Sumit, just for a day's darshan and another time when my cousin Priti and Prita were there. I remember that particular visit for reaching Shirdi as late as 2am.

There's something else that I remember from those times. I remember how my love for Sai Baba would take me to Shirdi but my addiction would make me drink there too in the evenings. Many a times, I had thought of taking a break from drinks for at least a day. But by the time it would be evening, those thoughts would succumb to my cravings.

I am almost sober for over two years now. It's normal to NOT get those cravings anymore, but I haven't forgotten about that phase of my life.

2

THE JOURNEY

I need an hour at least to get ready once I wake up in the morning. This morning was no exception. I was up at 2:30am, to shower and leave for the airport at 3:45am. I also managed enough time to have a delicious South Indian breakfast before boarding my flight at 05:00am. Unbelievably, there was no fog. Through the past week, all morning flights had been getting delayed by at least 2-3 hours, thanks to heavy fog. I was prepared for the same this morning too, but then, Baba's miracles work their magic. In fact, I had informed my cousin Tanu to be prepared for the delay.

Tanu, residing in Mumbai, is also a Sai devotee. About 4-5 years ago, he had told me once, "Whenever you plan a trip to Shirdi on the weekend, just ping me. I have a habit of looking for reasons or lack of it to visit Shirdi at any time. I would love to be there with you." Since I was indeed visiting on a weekend this time, there was no missing the mandated ping. Tanu immediately planned a drive to Shirdi with me in his car.

After I boarded the aircraft, I pinged Tanu. Apart from flight timings, one more important message had to be communicated to him. This was about my second round of breakfast. I was certain that I would be hungry when I landed and I had already concluded that grabbing some Mumbai Paw Bhaji (a red tangy curry served with fluffy, buttered buns) at the airport itself would be a fine idea. Before putting my phone on airplane mode, I called up my mother. It doesn't matter how old we are, Moms still need information about our safe travel.

Necessary phone calls done, mobile was put on airplane mode, it was time to get some sleep when the flight got airborne. I had barely closed my eyes for a few minutes when I heard a soft voice, "Mr. Khandelwal".

"Oh damn. I am sure she's here to reprimand me for taking off the mask", I thought to myself. The 'New Normal' requires us to wear masks at all times in the flight. I wish all such new rules could take into account the discomfort that I (and probably many others) feel with the mask. I was mentally ready to be reminded of the rules when the beautiful airhostess handed over a Veg Sandwich and a tetra-pack of mango juice to me and said softly, "Enjoy".

I looked at the sandwich and thought of the sumptuous South Indian breakfast I had eaten in Kolkata and the amazing Paw Bhaji I was about to devour at Mumbai. "No, this sandwich is not fitting in", my stomach cribbed. I decided against taking a bite. The best way to 'Enjoy' that sandwich was to NOT eat it. "I'd rather enjoy a nap", I realized decided.

The Journey

It's a tricky exercise to find a comfortable posture in the flight seat for a good nap. But I managed it just fine. I don't know when exactly I had drifted into sleep, but when I woke up suddenly and took a look at the watch, it showed 8:00am. I peeped outside, as much as I could from my aisle seat, hurriedly. My eyes were still sleepy, barely half open, but I could see that it was bright sunny outside. I could also see some trees below. I remembered that the arrival time was 8:05am and suddenly I felt a sense of urgency. I started looking for my new blue pair of shoes in a rush to get ready for arrival. After wearing them, I peeped out of the window again to see how much we had descended. Surprisingly, I saw no difference. That's when I figured, those 'trees' were actually clouds.

"How can we be flying so high, less than 5 minutes before the scheduled touchdown?" I wondered. Perplexed, I looked at my watch again, this time with eyes wide awake. I laughed at myself when I saw the correct time: 7:00am. I thought of going back to sleep, but my sleep was now broken for good. I had nothing much to do. In that still moment, I found something in my heart... deep, strong, pure, beautiful. It was gratitude.

I decided to write!

"Now I am on board and shall land in a few minutes"!

3

TOUCHDOWN – MUMBAI, DESTINATION – SHIRDI

A pleasant surprise awaited me in Mumbai. I was in the city after quite some time, but the airport looked so different. The Mumbai airport always looked like an ever-growing airport to me. Every time I travelled to Mumbai, I saw the airport a little bigger and more decorated. But this seemed like a completely new world to me. Upon asking people I understood that this was the New Terminal of the Mumbai airport. In view of the pandemic, only this terminal was operational in the city.

Everything looked different and unfamiliar, but I managed to grab a plate of my favourite Paw Bhaji. Tanu had presumed a delay and was yet to arrive to receive me at the airport. This gave me some extra time to relish my favourite snack.

After finishing my food, I walked to the pickup point. I had already texted Tanu my whereabouts, but wasn't sure when he'd reach the airport exactly. I was ready for a longer wait, but in a few minutes only, I heard his voice calling my name. As I loaded my luggage in his car, I wondered if he had come alone. I remember him telling me the previous night that his wife, Nidhi, would be coming along too. But she was not in the car. Just when I was wondering if all was okay at his home, I saw Nidhi walking up to the car.

Smiles and pleasantries exchanged, we got into the car and the wheels rolled for Shirdi. We chatted about everything and anything: city, family, business, professional matters, personal matters, intellectual and spiritual matters, just about anything. Amidst all these, I didn't care to notice how far we had reached through the infamous city traffic of Mumbai, until I realized that we were in Bhiwandi.

"Hey this is Bhiwandi. You know Dutta's, right?" I asked Tanu excitedly.

"What's that?" Tanu responded, looking visibly confused.

This was less of a surprise and more of a shock for me, that I knew about the yummy Dutta *Vada Paw* (the Indian version of the burger) in Tanu's city, but he was clueless. Many years ago, Sumit had taken me there, when it was a small outlet with a tin-ceiling, making only Vada Paw. Over time, it made a mark with its taste and quality. Today Dutta Vada Paw is not just big and famous, they serve over fifty varieties of fresh and packed items.

This is just the kind of success stories that I love.

It was easy to find Dutta Vada Paw on Google maps to stop by for this yummy Mumbai delicacy. After Paw Bhaji, I checked another box in my head: Vada Paw. Just when we were about to resume our drive, I received a call from Suchandra, the Asst. HR Manager of our company. "Sir, there is a candidate just apt for the post of ASM for Bihar. He has passed two rounds of interviews already and is highly recommended. Can you please take a final round of interview and close him today?"

It was a conscious break from work for a day, for this much desired trip. I was already in a relaxed mood, the spicy Vada Paw which had just been devoured, made me feel even more laid back. I really didn't feel like taking an interview at that time. I was in two minds, but then I realized, I can take a leave from office, but not from my responsibilities. I decided not to delay this any further. Once we got into the car, I connected to Zoom, finished the interview and closed him.

Mumbai to Shirdi is a pretty long drive. Near about half way to Shirdi, one has an option of taking a short cut through the single lane 'Ghoti Road', a route that I was very familiar with. I had driven to Shirdi many times before through that Ghoti road. As we were approaching the junction, Tanu reminded us that the road condition of that route was extremely bad. The second option we had was a longer route through Nashik. "It's better we take the Nashik route", he suggested.

Another round of Googling started. Nidhi was the official navigator and a very good one at that. The route through

Nashik was smoother but longer. It took us more than six hours to reach Shirdi. The short cut through Ghoti Road could have easily reduced this drive time by at least 1 to 1½ hours, had the road been motorable in good condition.

As we approached Shirdi, I felt some butterflies in my stomach.

4

CHANGE, UNCHANGED

The Mandir, I knew, would show up on our left as we were driving from Mumbai. Crowd started showing up as we approached the temple. The first sight of the Mandir was sprinkled with sights of hawkers, as always. Sitting on the road with flowers, candles, incense sticks, pictures of Sai Baba, they call out every devotee, offering to sell something or the other. There is always a good number of children amongst these hawkers, who even run after the devotees, desperately trying to sell whatever they have in their hand. Beggars are a common sight too.

"Those familiar little things. Nothing has changed."

I looked on the right side of the lane. Nothing was different here either. The lane was lined with shops selling all kinds of merchandise of Sai Baba, or flowers and prasaad for offerings. There were eateries, travel agent booths, hotels, all named with different variants of Sai. The nondescript guava sellers, the taxis and autos waiting for customers, the hawkers, the shop-owners, everyone seemed busy and calm at the same time, doing something or the other.

My watch showed the time as 3:40pm. We had booked our Darshan Pass for 4pm. Shirdi wasn't the same like it was three years ago. The Mandir of course was the same, but the systems had undergone a sea of change.

We found a parking soon. We took off our shoes inside the car and started walking towards the Mandir barefoot. It was a broken stretch of around 100 meters up to the road. There were small stones and pebbles all over the muddy terrain that hurt our feet, but we walked on, carefully dodging them. Just across the road from where we were was Gate No 1 where devotees had queued up for Darshan. We crossed the road and joined the queue. The crowd seemed to be more than what Prita and Rishi had mentioned to me. But then, it was the weekend, so I wasn't surprised.

Masks, as expected, was mandatory to enter the temple. Our body temperatures were also checked at the entrance. Auto dispensers were installed at the gates to ensure sanitization of hands also. There weren't many people inside the temple.

I noticed the changes in the system. As we entered the Mandir premises, there was a flowing water body in which we dipped our feet and rubbed it dry on jute mats on the way into the temple. The queue of the devotees was diverted via Dwarkamai to reach the main hall. We didn't have to wait anywhere until we reached the queue near the main hall.

We went through Dwarkamai to see Baba's 'dhuni', the fire that Baba himself had lit over 100 years ago, the fire that still burns as an immortal proof of His divine presence in our lives. I could relate everything to the series on Sai Baba that I have been watching. I watch Dwarkamai on my TV screen in the series Mere Sai daily, but seeing it in person was a completely different experience. Dwarkamai is the name of the home where Sai Baba lived for most of his life. This did not have covered walls earlier. It was in fact a deserted place that Sai chose to live at and spend his life in service to mankind. His ways of teaching and His preaching were different. Even till date, no one knows about the religion of Sai. He taught the value of life in his own spiritual ways, not in religious ways. The miraculous ways in which Sai Baba healed and protected His devotees cannot be explicitly described. No words can define Him precisely or describe him enough. He never claimed to be any God, but always emphasized that He is a messenger of God. Allah Malik (God's Wish) and Ramji Bhala Kare (God Bless You) were His patent ways to shower His love and blessings. He would often say to all his devotees "Sabka Malik Ek" (all Gods are the same. There's only One God for all.)

Entry inside Dwarkamai was restricted. We were only allowed to take a look from outside. I moved with the queue inside the Dwarkamai premises to reach the main Darshan hall. I couldn't wait to get a glimpse of my Sai.

5

DARSHAN – FINALLY

The moment was finally coming true. I was finally meeting my Sai after years.

There was a strange kind of anxiousness inside me as I walked to the main Darshan hall. But the moment I saw Sai Baba, that feeling vaporized. But there was another kind of a strange feeling. I felt as if it was no big deal. "I see Him daily", I thought. I couldn't understand why I felt that way.

The process of Darshan was simple and quick. In fact, it was so smooth and quick that we completed the entire process of Darshan and came out of the Mandir in just twenty minutes. I got to be in front of Baba, looking at His face, for not more than a minute. "Probably I couldn't connect with Him. I don't feel anything special about being either at Dwarkamai, or at the main Mandir. Nothing at all", I thought. At that moment, it seemed like watching Him on the series in the comfort of my home was much better.

I came out of the mandir with these strange thoughts clouding my head. We went back to the car, wore our slippers and entered a food joint nearby to have some food. Tanu and Nidhi had left their kids back in Mumbai, so they had to return back to Mumbai that very day. Tanu went to drop me to the hotel before leaving for Mumbai.

As we entered my Hotel, Sun and Sand, I realized that the Hotel didn't change even a bit. This was the only hotel I had stayed at in Shirdi, barring one instance, when this hotel itself was going through a renovation. I felt the same warm, welcome coziness at the lobby and at the beautiful garden. The quality of their service and food had always brought us back to that hotel again and again. I am sure that Shirdi has better hotels too, but this hotel made me feel at home. I took Tanu and Nidhi for a tour of the backyard to give them a glimpse of the beautiful swimming pool and lovely garden. I have many memories of spending time at these spots. After they left, I went up to my room.

Room No. 206 it was. I have stayed in this room before.

I entered the room and my eyes fell on the sofa on the left. I remembered how I sneaked in miniature bottles of whiskey to drink, even though it was strictly not allowed in the hotel.

I was a different person in those days, I wouldn't bother about anything. I had lost the connection between my heart and my mind. My compulsive mind would make me do things that I couldn't resist. I obeyed the dictates of the mind like a puppet. My mind, back then, was running on the wheels of "SELF WILL RUN RIOT". Wrongs would seem right and if anyone tried to show me the way and the right would feel like an unwanted lecture coming from some fool. Now, after overcoming that phase and being in sobriety, I have the wisdom to know the difference between right and wrong. This wisdom too, I believe, is Baba's grace.

I shook myself out of those memories and started unpacking. It was time to rest and relax for a few minutes. Around 6:15pm, I thought of calling up Mr. Dimre to check for the pass for Kakkar Aarti.

"Hello Mr. Dimre. How are you? I am Sujay from Kolkata. Remember, I had called you two days ago regarding the passes for Kakkar Aarti?"

"Hello Mr. Sujay. Yes, I remember." Mr Dimre replied courteously.

"I need your help to get the pass for tomorrow."

"It's only available online, but it is sold out", he replied.

My heart sank a bit, but I was certain about attending the morning Aarti.

"No worries. Earlier also I had attended Kakkar Aarti without booking a pass. I'll go in the general queue". I replied.

"But Sir, currently due to Covid-19 restrictions, no one is allowed inside for the Aarti without a pass." Dimre's voice pierced my heart this time.

What the hell is this new system now?

In a moment, it felt like I had lost something extremely valuable. I lost all hope upon hearing Dimre's words. The purpose of coming to Shirdi was lost in a moment. My energy seemed to take a nosedive. I kept requesting him to find a way to let me into the Mandir for the Aarti. He was on the computer. He informed me that 2 slots were still empty.

"Just 40 people are allowed in for the Aarti currently. 2 slots are still left, so please try online. I cannot help you", he announced.

My hopes rose again. I pleaded him again to help me.

"Call me at 8:30pm", he instructed and hung the call.

With hope in my heart and revived energy, I resumed my efforts to book the pass online for the next day.

13th December, 2020! That's the booking date I needed. The app disabled that option for me.

Damn, 2020. It can't stop challenging us again and again.

I immediately decided to call up Prita, who had introduced me to Mr. Dimre. I narrated my problem to her, briefed her about the conversation I had with Mr. Dimre.

"Wait. Let me speak to him and try."

She hung up.

I prayed for luck silently.

In five minutes, she called me back.

"I think, he can arrange but seems like he wants some money." Prita shared her observation.

"Let him take whatever money he wants. All I want is a pass for the Kakkar Aarti. I have stayed back in Shirdi for the night just to witness the Aarti." My hopes skyrocketed.

I a few minutes, Dimre called up.

"You come to Gate No 1 asap. I will arrange a pass for you." Dimre's voice sounded like music to my ears.

I felt a rush of the energy in my body and mind. I felt happy like never before.

"How much do I need to pay you, Sir?" I asked him.

"The charge is ₹600", he said.

I was more than comfortable hearing about the nominal charges for the service and huge help that he was providing me. I agreed to meet him at Gate 1 and hung up.

With a heartfelt gratitude I texted Prita:

"Looks like you have fixed everything here"

6

JUST MY LUCK(S)

I rushed to the hotel lobby to ask the *darban* (security guy) for a free drop to the Mandir. The hotel, I knew, provided this service. In just a few minutes, the driver dropped me there in the hotel car. I remembered to take his visiting card before he left so that I could call him back to pick me up. Soon, a few calls from Gate no 1 got me the clearance from the gate to enter the PRO office area. There was one guy already at the counter. I stood behind him in queue. A fear shot through me at that very moment: *What if this guy takes away my pass and I don't get the chance to attend the Aarti?* That feeling of insecurity numbed me for a moment. That wait behind the person at the counter for a few minutes felt like years.

After he left, I approached the counter and spoke through the small window.

"Hi. My name is Sujay", I tried to sound as audible as possible through the small opening in the glass window.

A gentleman in a white shirt sitting at the back of the room stood up. He was bald, but had thick black moustache. "Are you Mr. Khandelwal from Kolkata?", he asked.

"Yes. Are you Mr. Dimre?", I asked as a matter of fact. He nodded in response.

It felt good to finally meet the person who had given me first the worst, and then the best news a while ago. After exchanging the formal smiles, he looked into the computer screen at the counter. "Only 2 are left", he reconfirmed. "*Inko ek de do*" (give this person one), he instructed his colleague at the counter.

There are few things in life that you can't put into words, like the sense of joy I felt at that moment. I breathed a sigh of relief as my Aadhar (an identity proof) got scanned and I happily posed for the webcam. I think, they don't capture such smiling faces easily. Not to forget, the non-touch protocols they adhered to, in times of such pandemic, impressed me.

Formalities complete, it was time to have the pass in my hand. The guy looked into the computer screen and said, "₹600/-". I paid the money happily and collected my pass. As I was about to move away from the counter, I glanced at the pass which had an amount of ₹600 printed on it. I realized that I had only paid him the actual amount of the pass. I instantly remembered what Prita had mentioned over the call, about him expecting some money probably for his services. I asked him, what else I could do for him to return his kind favour.

"*Bas, madam ko call karke inform kar dena*", (nothing, just call and inform madam) he replied with a smile.

I couldn't believe it. Both Prita and I had misjudged him. We were completely wrong to assume that he was expecting money in return for his help. In reality, his intentions were as pure as a flower. He just wanted to help, not earn some extra bucks. When did a flower expect anything in return for its beautiful fragrance?

I began to realize Baba's plans all over again and my heart was once again filled with the deep sense of gratitude. I couldn't believe what I was experiencing. I became still, I couldn't move away from the counter. I stood there for a while, my hands folded in gratitude, my head slightly bowed with respect for him. Just a while ago, I had lost all hope but deep inside I had believed that I would be inside the temple to witness what I had come to see: The Kakkar Aarti. I would be forever grateful to the man who made it possible for me.

The joy of holding the pass in my hand and realizing that I would finally get to see the Kakkar Aarti brought a new burst of energy in me. I wish I could find a mirror nearby to see the way my eyes sparkled. The fatigue of the 6hour long drive was completely gone. I felt fresh and lively, like I had just woken up from a good, long sleep.

My work was done there. I had got my pass. It was time to get back to the hotel. I started moving towards the exit when I found an empty queue towards the Mandir. Darshan was still open. I checked my watch, it was 8:00pm. I asked the security guy, "*Bhaiya*, can I go inside now?" He looked at me and took a quick look at my hand which held the pass. "Yes", he said, but instructed me to take off my slippers and deposit off my mobile. "Of course. I am coming back in a moment", I assured him and rushed to do the needful towards the nearby mobile and slipper deposit counters. My excitement and happiness knew no limits. But when I returned back to the queue, something struck me. The guard was standing in a place under dim lights from where I couldn't see his face clearly.

Did he misunderstand the pass in my hand to be of the current darshan? I wondered.

Indeed, my guess was right. I showed him my pass and he agreed that it was not the right one for the current darshan. The confusion was sorted. I thanked him and moved out of the queue without thinking twice.

I went back to collect my belongings and started strolling. I had walked only a few steps aimlessly when a random thought came to me. *Let me go towards the back side of the temple, near Gate No. 3. May be, I could buy some stuff.*

The back side of the temple is lined with shops. I knew the route towards Gate 3 like the back side of my hand. I started walking, took a turn through the lane to reach the shops. The very first glance fell on a particular shop which was situated high up on the elevated row. It was the very shop from where Riya and I had once bought lots of books, DVDs and pictures of Sai Baba, many years ago.

A strange feeling occurred to me. It felt like she was right there beside me, reminding me of the music we had heard that morning when we had completed the Kakkad Aarti. I felt the soothing effect of witnessing the Aarti, the peace gelling into my senses, making me feel completely calm and blissful. I felt blessed to be at Shirdi again and that I was going to witness the Kakkar Aarti again. As I remembered my previous visits, I recalled that some shops open as early as 5am. As much as I wanted to cherish the memories of my previous visits to those shops, I realized that it was getting late. I had to finish another important task I had in hand: making donations on behalf of the devotees who had sent their donations through me.

Anyone who is a frequent visitor to any temple in India would know of this age-old tradition of sending donations. For the longest time known to humankind, we have believed that the greatest of all deeds is to contribute in some way for the larger good. Temples and religious places have always played a prominent role in working towards the greater cause. Shirdi Sai Sansthan is no different. The Trust runs schools, colleges, hospitals, clinics, shelters for the homeless and a bunch of other things that truly add value to the society at large. Just near the temple itself, the free food distribution center feeds thousands of poor people 365days a year. So, whenever someone visits Shirdi, it's a common practice that many others send donations through him or her. No one likes to let go of an opportunity to donate for the good work, that has the divine blessings of Mere Sai.

I knew that most of the donation counters are inside the temple, but I found one outside too. I made the donations against receipt and collected Baba's prasaad in the form of Udi packets. (For those new to 'UDI', it is the holy ash from the Dhuni, the fire that was lit by Baba, the one that still is burning at Dwarkamai.)

Udi is one thing which Sai used to give to everyone. He cured different problems with this holy ash, almost like magic. Even today, Udi is believed to have the power to heal any and every problem related to mind, body or soul. Udi has a great significance for all Sai devotees, For the ones who believe in Sai, it is most valuable. I have been carrying a packet of Udi from Shirdi for years, but I haven't opened it yet. Baba has been so kind enough to help me without even me having to open the packet. It remains always, in a secret pocket of my wallet.

Satisfied on the completion of this work, I started towards Dwarkamai, Baba's home, where he had spent most of his life and took his Mahasamadhi.

7

THE DIVINE & HIS MIRACLES

Dwarkamai was closed and could not be accessed from the usual gate. Currently due to Covid-19, it could be accessed only through the darshan line while entering the darshan hall.

But luckily, I could enter the Chawri, as it was open to free access.

Chawri is right opposite Dwarkamai, near the entry of Gate No.3. I have been to the Chawri many times before but this time was different. There have been many times when we have done prasaad distribution right at the chowk in front of Dwarkamai and Chawri. I remembered those times vividly.

This time however was different. Thanks to the pandemic, there was no way to organize such distribution. Somehow, I liked the moment: no rush, no worry, no hurry. I was all by myself and yet I was completely okay with that. There was a certain calm in that moment that I could absorb and feel deep within. It seemed like I was fully, wholeheartedly there. It's not easy to describe that feeling in words, but I felt it all.

The darshan of Sai I had managed a few hours ago was such a brief one. I could feel that I had not connected to Sai yet. I entered the Chawri, sat there for a moment and looked up. On all the four walls around me, pictures of Sai were painted. Each picture depicted scenes from the time when Sai lived there. Each picture showed something about Sai's daily life.

I felt like I knew these moments too well. I got up and started taking a good look at each of the pictures. In some picture, He was speaking to his disciples, in another one, He was feeding the *dhuni*. The moments felt so real that I couldn't help wondering how could I connect so well with them. That's when I remembered why I felt so deeply connected to those moments depicted in the pictures. I had seen them all in the television series MERE SAI.

For over 6 months now, my evening routine comprises of watching a few episodes of MERE SAI, a serial that captures the life and miracles of Sai. I feel so grateful that my friend, Gaurav, who himself is a Sai devotee, helped me download the app to facilitate this daily routine. The series has answers to anything and everything. It doesn't matter what the doubts and questions in my head are on any given day, I get answers to all my questions, that too almost instantly while watching the recorded series. Yes, for most people it could possibly be nothing more than just a serial for entertainment purposes, but for me, it is a part of my day when I connect with Sai's divine presence. When I watch the serial, I don't see actors, I see Sai and the people who were fortunate to meet him in his lifetime. I live every moment in the story that I see on screen.

I spent a few more moments over there, soaking in the essence that were captured in the pictures. Then I decided to click some on my own phone. I got out and clicked the empty chowk where we used to do prasad distribution. Memories came rushing back to me again. I remembered distributing Halwa, Chirwa, Khichari and Puri Sabzi (name of few Indian sweets and snacks) along with my wife Riya over there. Each of those memories reminded me of Baba's blessings in my life. He always prompted us to do *seva* (service to others) with our hands. I remembered a girl named Pinki, to whom we used to place orders for our *prasaad* distribution. For many years, all we had to do was call her every time we visited Shirdi and place our order. She would sweetly take down the details of whatever we wished for and deliver them duly as per our request. She would help us with the distribution too. I fondly remember her sweet nature and her voice that radiated her smile over the phone too.

Later, she took up a full-time job and got busy, unable to take orders. There is no single soul who has not received the grace of Sai for being a part of *seva* in Shirdi in some way or the other. I blessed her silently in my heart and moved on.

Suddenly, a thought came into my mind.

I have three large pictures of Sai, adorning the walls of my house in Kolkata, which were bought in 2013-2014 from a particular shop nearby. I decided to take a look into the same shop.

The lane is full of shops on the left side with almost the same stuff being sold in every one of them. From pictures, idols, decorations, key rings, bracelets, books, garlands, cloths for Sai, these shops sold a wide variety of items. Sai Baba's *murtis* (idols) of different sizes and postures are the top attraction in these shops, closely followed by Sai's pictures. You name a size and shape and you will get it. One is truly spoilt for choice in these shops.

On my right was the backside of the mandir with a high wall and a boundary. From this point, only the tomb of the Mandir is visible. I looked at the tomb and got goosebumps. The tomb was shining like gold, glistening like never before. I realized that this place remains so crowded usually that I had never noticed this view before. A few pictures were clicked instantly.

I started feeling a bit restless to meet Baba in the morning. The more I kept looking at His tomb, the more I had butterflies in my stomach. Whether it was anxiety or excitement, I couldn't tell. I clicked a few more pictures, once again silently thanked Baba for the moment and moved on. I was yet to locate the shop from where I had bought the pictures during my previous visits.

It's not an easy task in this lane to locate any specific shop, given that they all look alike. I knew, it would not be easy to spot my shop after all these years, but here too I found some help. There was a renovation work going on, on the frontal side of the building housing all these shops. In a way, no shop was distinguishable. But this forced me to pay more attention and look more keenly. I remember how we had spent over an hour in that shop, selecting the three beautiful pictures which are now in my home. I wanted to be sure that I go to the exact same shop I had been to years ago with my wife. In no time, I found it.

I didn't have any specific plan of purchasing anything in particular. Then why did Baba bring me in that shop? I wondered. I immediately wanted to buy a small picture of Sai Baba to be kept on my office table. I looked through various options and almost finalized one. But Sai had some other plans for me.

Just when I was going to pay for my purchase, I happened to casually glance at the wall on the other side where all the big pictures were hanging on the wall. You name a colour or you ask for a size, they have it all. My heart wished for another big picture.

I looked through the variety of pictures displayed. A picture where Baba was in a green turban attracted me a lot, so did another golden one. Finally, after a while, I settled for a medium size wall mounting picture. It was not green or golden, but rather a pink one, a vibrant, beautiful pink. I had already decided to put it on the wooden panel of my cabin in the office.

As I made the payment, I struck up a conversation with the shopkeeper. I expressed my gratitude to him for the three older pictures that I had bought from his shop, the ones that grace my home today. There is no corner of Shirdi that I hadn't visited before, yet I ended up asking him, *"Bhaiya, prasaad kahaan se loon?"* (Brother, where do I buy the prasaad from?)

The shopkeeper replied: *"Bhaiya, aap A S Gangwal mein chale jao. Waha jaake bolna Panhale wale pere ke liye."* (Brother, you go to the shop named A S Gangwal. Once you reach there, ask for the Panhale make of sweets). The sweets were low on sugar and very tasty, he informed.

'Wow, this was new', I thought. I followed his instructions and went to A. S. Gangwal. The shopkeeper was right. When I reached there and tasted them, I agreed that they were super yum. I placed order for several boxes of those sweets. I stood there patiently, waiting for over 30 mins to get them packed as the number of boxes were quite many.

I already had the pictures of Baba in my hand which I had bought some time ago, now I had the boxes of prasaad too. I balanced the picture of baba on one hand and the boxes of prasad in another and walked towards the road. It didn't take me long to call the hotel car. The hotel car brought me back to the hotel soon.

As soon as I reached the hotel, I headed to the reception to confirm the pick-up timings for Kakkar Aarti for the next morning. I couldn't wait to be at the temple, especially after the way I managed to procure the pass, that too when only two were remaining. I wouldn't miss the Aarti for anything, I thought.

At the reception I was told that I had to be at the temple at least a few minutes before 03:30AM. "The gates close at 3:30am, Sir. So, you have to be there before that", they confirmed. I had witnessed the Kakkar Aarti several times before and was aware about these timings. I smiled as the receptionist went about explaining the rules to me meticulously. I guess, from my face, they could tell that I was already aware of the rules. I only wanted to confirm the availability of the hotel car service for my trip to the temple at that hour. They assured me about it.

Happy and content, I took the elevator to go back to my room and call it a day.

8

THE MIRACLE MORNING

It was about 10pm when I reached my room. I felt tired and exhausted and wanted to sleep as soon as possible, but some work was still pending. As much as I wish I could avoid them, I settled down and embarked upon completing some important calls.

By the time I finished the calls, it was already 11:15PM. I didn't realize it would take so much of time, but what had to be done, had to be done.

When I looked at the time, it got me a bit worried. I knew, I had to wake up by 02:30am at least to get ready and leave for Kakkar Aarti. This meant, I had far less time for a good night's sleep. I knew my challenge after all. I always take minimum 45 minutes time to get ready after I wake up in the morning.

"What if I fail to wake up on time?", I had the worst thought that could have got at that time. I decided to set an alarm loud and clear, lest my fears come true.

The smartphone these days perform the task of an alarm clock also. I set the alarm and kept the phone on the side table. It was time to get some much-needed sleep. I usually don't take too long to fall asleep, but somehow, in spite of my best efforts, sleep eluded me at that time. I think it was due to my underlying worry that I wouldn't manage to wake up on time. The more I tried desperately to fall asleep, the more I struggled to fall asleep.

May be, I should book a wake-up call!

As I warmed up in my blanket, I remembered this sure shot way to be certain that I woke up on time. I had done it zillion times before. I looked at the phone set at the other end of the room. I had used this very phone before, during my trips with Riya, to book wake up calls from the reception. "This will definitely keep me on time", I thought.

But even though I had this great idea, the distance between the bed and the phone seemed to be in miles on this cold winter night.

No, nothing is taking me out of the blanket now.

I dropped the idea of booking a call from the reception at that very moment and tried to sleep.

Just when I closed my eyes, I had a thought that my mobile could be in silent mode.

Damn. How could I not check that?

I immediately reached out for my mobile. To my relief, the phone was not on silent mode. Once again, I checked the alarm, put my phone on the bed side table and finally drifted into sleep, relaxed and assured.

Beep... Beep... Beep....

I was still in my sleep when I heard my phone alarm ring. The sound seemed too distant initially, but it grew louder. It was time to wake up.

Still groggy and half asleep, I picked up my phone. The alarm had gone off at the right time. The clock read 02:30am. As I pressed a button on my phone to stop the alarm, I was happy to have woken up on time. It felt good to know that in a short while, I would be headed to the mandir.

It felt good to be in Shirdi.

It felt good to come to Shirdi after years.

It felt good to remember that I was about to witness that Kakkar Aarti again after a while.

Still in my thoughts, I stuck my hand out of the blanket and picked up the phone again to check the time. Barely five minutes must have passed since I had stopped the alarm from beeping. I looked at the time:

03:50 AM

WHAT???????

Something shook me up so hard that I felt like a 1000volts of electric shock had struck me.

I couldn't believe what I was seeing. I must have slept after switching off the alarm, but I didn't quite remember falling asleep. I had no memory of the time in between. What happened between 02:30–03:50AM, Sai alone knows.

But I didn't have time to think about anything. It felt like I had lost everything in my life. Shivers ran down my body. I felt fear, anxiety, helplessness, hopelessness and a mix of hundred other things that I can't even define. It was something that I had never felt before in my life. I was supposed to report at the Mandir gate at 3.30 am. The gate was supposed to close at that very time only. I cursed myself so much when I remembered this.

How could I miss the alarm? How on earth could I fall asleep again?

I don't know what happened, but all of a sudden, I felt a sudden, magical surge of energy in my body. It seemed like I had suddenly been touched by a magic wand and gifted with multitasking abilities. I jumped out of the bed, lit a cigarette and called the driver as I sat on the toilet. "Bhaiya, I am late. DO you think the mandir gates would be open right now to let me in?" A gentle voice answered me over the speaker of the phone kept aside in the toilet. "Sai only knows, Sir. But you can try", the driver replied in the calmest tone.

"Start the car, I am coming", I blurted out and got into action. In the next few minutes, I brushed my teeth, changed into the jeans hanging on the rack, wore my slippers, grabbed my wallet and other necessities and rushed out of the room. I ran down the staircase without waiting for the elevator. The car was waiting for me.

When I sat in the car, my watch read 03:56AM. My body was still warm, I was wearing the same T-Shirt in which I was sleeping under the blanket, barely 6 minutes ago. *"Bhaiya, jitna jaldi ho sakey chalao"* (Brother, drive as fast as you can), I told the driver.

I have no memory of leaving home on any day of my life before 30 minutes from my wake-up time. On an average, I take roughly 45-50 minutes to get ready. So generally, I never get out of the house before an hour of me leaving my bed. But I did that, in 6 minutes flat. Sai alone knows how it happened.

I could still feel the tension in every cell of my body. I felt claustrophobic, I could feel my own heavy breath. I rolled down the window of the car to get some fresh air and ease myself out. But the cold breeze of the early hours of a winter morning nearly froze me. I kept looking at my watch. I wanted time to stop till I reached the gates of the temple. I prayed for the gates to remain open anyhow. I wished at that moment, I had the power to hold time still for some moments, at least till I managed my entry to the temple.

The car reached gate No1. There was not a soul around except for the lone security guard. I literally jumped out of the car and ran towards the gate to cross the railings. But that moment, something happened. My ribs made a blunt, bony sound.

I felt a stabbing, unbearable pain in my ribs! I had got a bad muscle cramp.

Moments ago, I was in severe tension. My body was still warm when I had got into the car but I had suddenly come in contact with the cold breeze. The cramp could be a result of this sudden change. I knew at that moment itself that had it been any other day, I would have sat down there itself, nursing my excruciating pain. No one other than Riya knows how these cramps, at one point in life, had become a nagging trouble for me. Every time I had these cramps, I would go through unbearable pain which apart from me only she could feel and empathize. Earlier, the pain would often render me immobile, but at that moment, I was unstoppable. I put a hand on my ribs which was paining and just ran, like I had never run before. The time on my watch showed 03:59AM. The main Mandir entry door, where the security scan was to happen, was still about 300-400mts away. I kept running, with a single-minded focus: I had to meet my Sai, I had to see the Kakkar Aarti.

Just at the nick of time, I reached the gate. I showed my entry pass to the security personnel and got entry into the temple.

I glanced at my watch one last time.

The clock read 04:00am.

9

SAI, I AM HERE

My mind ran through the events of the previous ten minutes of my life.

Ten minutes ago, I had almost lost everything. I had no hope of reaching the temple. I felt helpless and hopeless in every sense of the words. Yet, here I was, feeling happy and joyful after the most stressful and painful ten minutes of my life.

I felt damn tired. My pulse rate probably had doubled from the running, even though it was barely for a few hundred meters. I tried to run the events through my mind, specially from the car to the mandir, from the moment I felt that stab in my rib to the time when I was inside the temple. I couldn't recollect anything. It seemed like a dark web, a maze that I was already out of, but didn't know how I managed to do it.

At that moment, I looked at Baba and at that very moment, I did what I have been waiting to do for the last 24hours: SURRENDER. I sat down, sweating, panting. My heart rate began to reduce, I began to feel easy with each breath. My eyes almost automatically went towards the clock hanging on the wall on the right-hand side.

04:05 AM!

I looked into Baba's eyes. My conversation began with HIM.

"Why this way Baba, why like this? What if I had slept for a minute more? Why are you trying these things out on me since last evening?"

I still don't know what prompted me to ask these questions to Baba at that time. What was I expecting?

But at that very moment, I felt as if Baba was talking to me.

Yes, My SAI was speaking to me. I heard His voice telling me, "You were too tired last night. I wanted you to get some extra sleep. You haven't slept well for two nights. You had a morning flight too. But why are you upset? Aren't you here now?"

Immediately, I had an eye contact with Baba. I couldn't have possibly expressed anything in words but my gratitude overflowed and I could tell, my SAI felt it all. He cares for me just like my mother cares for me. His love for me is similar to what I feel from my mother.

"Thank you so much Sai Baba, Thank You", the words flowed straight from my heart, overloaded with sincerest gratitude.

Still a bit overwhelmed, but well settled, I looked around. Since I was the last one to enter the temple, I got to sit at the end of the queue. There were four queues in all. Two on either sides of the hall and two in the middle. I had chosen to be in the middle and not on the ones at the sides. Even though the distance between me and Sai Baba was more here, I liked it here. There was no obstruction in between Him and me and that gave me a clear view, just like what I wanted.

At exactly 04.15 am, the rituals began with a loud *shankhnaad* (a sound generated while blowing into a conch shell). Soon after, the bhajans (devotional songs) followed. The song *Utha Utha O Sainath* (rise up, rise up, oh lord Sai) started playing. It was a Marathi song. As I listened to the bhajan, I could still feel the overflow of love and gratitude for Sai. Gradually, a few *sevakars* (servents) of Baba entered the main podium. I was totally immersed in the moment; I had no sense of time or urgency. I don't know when the clock struck 04.30am and the Aarti started, as always on precise time.

I took out the Aarti book which I bought the previous night. I had forgotten the lyrics of the *aarti* and I didn't feel great about it. There was a time, may be four years ago, when I knew every word of that Aarti song by heart. I used to visit the Sai Temple at Deshopriyo Park, Kolkata, every morning around 6.40AM. I would go daily, just to attend the Aarti. There, I could sing along easily without a book.

But in the past few years, I had lost the zeal to go to mandir. Eventually, even when I went to visit, it was for a Darshan only. But at that moment, in Shirdi, after 4 years, it was so very different. When the bhajan started, every word in the book seemed difficult to connect with. Yet the feel was superb.

With the book in one hand, I looked up to baba and felt as if he had disconnected with me altogether. All this while I was sitting on the ground like others while the Aarti was going on. After some time, I started feeling a knee pain, the pain that had developed in my body during the infamous lockdown.

I had been suffering from this pain since the 3rd month of the lockdown. I used to sit at one place with one leg folded under the other at the dining table of my house, working on my laptop for hours. Those days, everyone was working from home and I was no exception. I realized during that time that dining table isn't really the ideal place to work on, especially if you are required to sit at one place for hours. Those days were super hectic for me and my whole team. I was working for 12-14 hours each day. While the knee pain reminded me of the lockdown period, I had one more thing to thank Sai Baba for.

Our business didn't bite dust in the lockdown at all. Thank you, Sai. I whispered in my head; I am sure Sai Baba heard it.

I focused back into the moment.

On the rows on either side of the hall, people were standing in the queues, but the ones in our (the middle) rows were sitting. I don't know why I suddenly stood up, looked at baba and then again focused back to the book to follow the words of the bhajan. After just a couple of pages, I could fully connect to the Aarti. I realized that I didn't feel the need to read up each word anymore. I was holding the book in my hand still, but it was mostly just for reference only for a word here and there. I looked at Baba and felt the gratitude again.

I was the only one standing for a while now in the entire queue. While I was busy chanting the aarti, I saw a gentleman stand up in my queue 4-5 rows ahead of me. I didn't bother much. In few seconds, a security guy pointed at him and asked him to sit down. It was rather a strict and firm order, not a request, which made the gentleman sit down immediately in his place. I realized that it could be my turn next to be ordered by the security guard to sit down. I guess there couldn't have been a better view of Sai Baba from anywhere in the hall other than the one where I was standing. I was there straight in front of Baba, face to face with Him, separated only by devotees who were ahead of me, but seated. Immediately I cursed that guy who had stood up before me. I thought, because of him the security guy would make me sit down too. I realized that I would be able to look at baba even while sitting down, but the view which I was enjoying standing from there would not be the same. While my mind was evaluating all this, I decided not to have an eye contact with the security guy. I made up my mind that I would not look at him till he waves at me. Few minutes passes and I completely forgot all about this while I got engrossed in the aarti. Sai Baba had understood my knee and my heart condition, I guess. I remained standing there itself for the rest of the entire duration.

I felt like Baba had accepted me back. I felt as though Baba had forgiven me for all wrongs that I have done under the influence of alcohol. I felt gratitude flowing inside me, faster than the blood in my veins, reaching all parts of my body. It is a feeling that I doubt anyone can describe in words. I kept looking at Baba and every now and then at the words in the book, and sang along with the Aarti. There was a feeling of peaceful joy throughout the entire time, till the Aarti was completed around 5.05am.

10

TEARS OF DIVINE LOVE

Kakkad Aarti is certainly the most beautiful and one of the longest Aartis performed at Shirdi. Hundreds of people come from across the country to witness this Aarti (which currently allows limited people under the new rules formulated in view of the pandemic). It doesn't matter if the bhajans are in Marathi, people simply immerse in the divine energy that breaks through all language and culture barriers. The process of Kakkar Aarti includes the invocation of Sai, followed by giving him a bath with milk and water and then doing his *shringaar* (dressing him up). This is followed by more bhajans and chanting. Throughout the process, my eyes were glued to Baba. I had no sense of what was around me. I simply kept looking at him, watching him take a bath and get ready for the day.

After about another ten minutes, we were asked to leave the hall. The queue on the left started moving first. I knew, it was time for me to make a move too. This time, I did not feel disconnected and unheard, like the way I had felt the previous evening. Not only had I spent a good amount of time, but also felt the deep connection that I had been yearning for.

With that feeling of contentment, I moved towards the left side of the hall to join the queue that was moving towards Baba. The exit doors are towards the front of the hall. The moment I entered the channel marked out by a railing to join the line, something happened. I started getting goosebumps.

I was closer to Baba now but still at a distance. My eyes were fixated on his face, there was neither any disturbance, nor any obstruction. I felt a rush of deeper, divine connection. At that very moment when I crossed the pillar, my eyes started watering. With each step forward, I felt tears welling up in my eyes more and more. It was like a tide that refused to be tamed. I could feel divine grace and love in every cell of my body. I could feel the love growing with each passing moment. I started crying, overwhelmed with this magical realization of divine grace in my love. I cried like a little child who had just found his long-lost puppy. I cried, oblivious to the shouts of the security guards, screaming *"chaliye chaliye"* (Move fast move fast). It was a moment of ecstatic divinity, something that I had never felt before in my life.

I was still walking along with the crowd that proceeded steadily towards the exit. Finally, I was just next to Baba, right beside the podium where He sat on His throne. It was the closest that I could be to Baba physically. I bowed my head down to touch the white marble of the platform. The cold marble had the warmth of love and grace that only Baba can shower. I kept my head touched to the stone for a few moments. There is no joy as pure as being able to bow your head at Baba's feet. There is a marble imprint of Sai Baba's feet carved on another piece of marble. I stood up and touched "*Sai Charan*" (baba's feet) before finally proceeding to exit the mandir.

As I was leaving, I felt so very happy that I couldn't feel anything else except pure gratitude. I realized that I had no way to express that feeling. I knew only two words and those two words got stuck on my lips: "THANK YOU".

11

SHOWERS OF BLESSINGS

Anyone who knows the story of Shirdi Sai Baba would know the significance of the neem tree in the temple premises of Shirdi.

The Neem tree of Shirdi is of utmost significance because

It is under this tree that Sai Baba was first seen. He was barely a 16year old boy when the villagers of Shirdi saw him for the first time. No one knew about his childhood, no one knew his parents, no one knew where he came from. He simply sat there, defying heat or cold weather, asking for nothing, fearing nothing. The life of penance that the 16yr old boy lived amazed every villager.

Sai Baba lived under that Neem tree for years. He blessed and cured many ailments of people who came to him for relief. Even to this day, the Neem Tree is sacrosanct place in Shirdi. Devotees could earlier sit under the tree, that once provided shade to Sai Baba. But over the years, it became difficult to control the crowd gathering there.

The leaves of that Neem tree are considered to be auspicious. Earlier people would try to get the leaves of that plant by plucking them from the branch directly. But thereafter, the temple authorities decided to create a barricade around the tree to prevent the crowd from damaging the tree. Now, the only way one could get hold of a leaf was by collecting the ones which had naturally fallen on the white marble platform built around the tree. Needless to say, it's now a matter of luck to get a leaf as the number of devotees are thousand times more than the number of leaves that fall from the tree.

I wasn't going to leave without trying my luck.

After the beautiful experience I had at the Kakkar Aarti, I headed to the Neem Tree. There was very little crowd, I got a leaf and put it in my mouth happily.

I couldn't wait to get back to the hotel, freshen up and grab a cup of tea. In the rush at the early hour that morning, I hadn't got time to drink my morning tea. I came out of Gate No.1 on to the main road. I was still walking bare feet. My slippers were left in the car. I had taken them off just before I had jumped out to reach the temple at the nick of time. Had I left them at the counter, I could have collected them and worn them by now.

The plan was to cross the road and take an auto ride back to the hotel. Suddenly, out of the blue, I decided to walk.

I felt like walking through the familiar lanes. My wife Riya and I have walked through these lanes before, sometimes in the dark early-hours of the morning, sometimes at night.

Memories. Oh, such lovely memories.

It was a pleasant morning by then. People of all ages had begun to gather around the temple area. I looked at the crowd and remembered, it was a Sunday.

"That explains the swell in the crowd", I thought. On weekends, many people come to Shirdi from nearby areas at early hours to avoid the day-crowd.

I kept walking, my mind still running through the chain of events of the morning. I felt light and calm. I took a turn to reach the lane that had three left turns, all of which led straight to the hotel. I was walking a bit slowly and carefully since I was barefoot. I kept a watch on the walkway to avoid stones or glass pieces.

I could have taken the first left turn itself, but I kept walking. As I reached the second lane, a large signboard grabbed my attention. I looked at the board that stated in bold letters, "FREE DARSHAN PASS COUNTER THIS WAY". It was 05:30am already and I had asked the driver to report at the hotel at 7am. I was set to return back a couple of hours later and I definitely didn't intend to get late again. I was about to turn left and head to the hotel when I heard a voice from behind.

"Could you please tell me where to collect the entry pass from?", a very ordinary looking gentleman was asking me the question. These days, even for a regular darshan, one has to show his ID proof and get a pass to enter the temple. I turned around and showed him the sign board that I had seen a moment ago. The man proceeded towards the direction of the counter. I was about to resume my walk to the hotel when I heard a voice calling *"Aajao, aajao"* (come, come).

I turned around again, wondering who was calling. It was the security guard's voice. He was calling the gentleman who has just asked me for directions. The security guard was calling him to enter the queue to the temple even without a pass. I was amazed at his luck. While no one is allowed to enter the temple without a valid pass, which had to be obtained by showing some ID proof, here he was being called to go straight inside the temple without any formalities. Even while I was thinking about these things, the gentleman who had asked for directions was already heading towards the queue.

Without thinking anything, I asked the security guard, "Can I go too?" The guard didn't say a word. He simply nodded in approval.

The next moment, I was in the queue again, to get into the temple.

12

FROM CONNECT TO CONSCIOUSNESS

I had completely forgotten about the time and the plan I had for the morning. There was certainly some other force driving me at that moment.

After I entered the serpentine lanes built to channelize the crowd into the temple premises, I looked around aimlessly, not sure of why I was there again.

Why did I get inside again?
I have had my full darshan, even of the kakkad aarti.
There's not much time left for my departure from Shirdi.
The car would be at the hotel to pick me up in a short while.

Thoughts were too many, but none explained, why I was inside the temple again. After scrambling for an answer for a few moments, I gave up.

Jaisi teri ichcha Baba. (As you wish, Baba).

I realized that there must have been some divine plan in bringing me inside the temple again. I stopped worrying about the time or the urgency and decided to go with the flow. I just kept moving with the crowd. The queue stopped briefly at Gate No. 5 and then at Gate No. 4. I didn't bother about it.

My mind was absolutely blank. The incoherent chatter of the people around me didn't reach my ears, neither did the sound of birds or breeze. I just kept walking and walking.

Suddenly, I realized that I was standing inside Dwarkamai, in front of Baba's Dhuni. I have no clear memory of what had transpired between the time I entered the queue without the entry pass to the moment I was there in front of the Dhuni (except that the queue had stopped twice briefly).

There was something unusual about that moment. I looked at the dhuni and then, most casually looked around. That very moment, I experienced magic.

I stood motionless inside Dwarkamai, and watched the whole place glitter like gold. Every corner, every stone was shining like I had never seen before. I started getting goosebumps, I could feel something different, which I had never experienced during any of my previous trips to Dwarkamai before this day.

I remembered that I see this place on TV every day in "Mere Sai" serial. I saw the spots which I could associate with deeply. The door where Baba stood, the stone on which

Baba sat, the area where he spoke to people who visited him, everything was right there in front of me. The realization that I was actually in the place that was once Baba's abode, meant a huge deal to me. And then, it was the moment of another out-of-the-world experience.

I saw Sai Baba sitting right there on the stone, exactly how I saw him every evening on television. I couldn't take my eyes off Him, as I felt the rush of some unexplained energy in my body. It is an experience that I can never put into words. It would be a futile effort to try and define divinity in its truest, purest form. But I can definitely say that I had experienced it at that moment.

I immediately realized, why Sai had brought me back to the Mandir again. The previous evening, I could barely connect with Him when I was at this place. That morning also, I had skipped visiting Dwarkamai altogether. I was late and hence probably, driven straight to the mandir.

The Mandir was built on the *Samadhi Sthal* (the place where Baba was buried) at Buttywada, years after Baba left for the heavenly abode, as per Baba's advice. When Baba left his body behind, he had advised his disciples to bury Him here in October 1918. He had told Tatya and everyone else that His body would be there to protect them all. This is the reason, even today, the Mandir and the Samadhi-Sthal attracts pilgrims from across the globe in large numbers.

But DwarkaMai was the place where Baba had lived for most of his life. These walls of Dwarkamai are vibrant even today, warm in the heat of the Dhuni that Baba had lit. That's the place where I could feel him at that moment. I could feel him in each and every piece of item that I saw around me. Nothing seemed lifeless. The inanimate objects seemed to be throbbing with divine energy. The more I looked around, the more familiar they appeared to me. The intensity of the connection was so strong that I felt that I had come here a thousand times before. The experience was more powerful than anything I had ever experienced in my life.

I stopped questioning, why I was there and why Baba got me to the temple again. A while ago, I was perplexed and confused, not sure why I was doing what I was doing. But here I was, drowning in the ocean of Baba's blessings and mercy. I realized that this itself was the first in my life, that I was in the temple for the third time during a single trip. I had made two visits to the temple several times before during my previous trips to Shirdi, but this was certainly a first.

13

GRACE OVERFLOWING

The connection that I was missing the previous day was finally regained. In fact, it was much more than just a mere connect. It was nothing short of consciousness of the presence of divine love and grace in my life.

I felt fantastic. There was no worry, no hurry, no discomfort or disconnect. I just felt blissful and joyous as I moved out of there.

I proceeded to the Samadhi Sthal to get Baba's darshan one more time. I wanted to thank him once again as I was immensely grateful for everything that He had given me in my life. I always knew that Baba's wishes were the driving forces in my life, but I had never experienced it so powerfully before than that moment.

I realized that off late I could literally feel his instructions in my head, guiding me at every juncture, showing me the way ahead. There was nothing in my life that was happening without Baba's will. My mind ran through the sequence of the magical moments I was having from the moment I had left Kolkata. None of them had any rhyme or reason, except for Sai's immense grace. "Thank you, Sai. Thank you for being my guiding force and protecting me always", I said with a broad smile, looking straight into His eyes.

Earlier when I was there in front of Baba, the *shringaar* was going on. But now it was complete. I looked at him from His head to His feet. He had worn a light pink robe with roses in two shades darker in pink. The pattern in which the roses were embroidered on the cloth displayed fine craftsmanship, worthy of admiration. It cannot be understood until seen from a close distance. Baba simply looked beautiful. I absorbed the visuals of Baba and his beautiful attire as deeply as I could to imprint the memory of that moment forever. My gaze was fixed on him in such a way that I had zero consciousness of anything else at that time. I was simply glued to him. In all honestly, even as I am writing this book, I am struggling to find words to describe how it felt at that moment.

Some moments later, I heard the guards screaming, "Chalo, chalo". It did not bother me. I was content with the time I had got to spend with Baba!

Finally, I had to leave and so I bent down as before to put my forehead on the white marble and stood up to touch Sai Charan. "Bring me back to Shirdi soon, Baba." I requested Him and finally moved out of the mandir.

I was certain that Baba would fulfill my wish soon.

I exited the mandir through the same door which I had taken in the morning after the Kakkar Aarti. It again brought me back to the blessed Neem Tree.

My eyes were trying to look for the nearest neem leaf lying on the floor across the guarded boundary. I was ready to bend down and lean forward to put my hands inside the railing to grab it.

There were quite a few leaves on the platform. I chose the nearest leaf which seemed easily reachable. But when I tried to get my hand through the barricade to get it, I couldn't reach it. It was still at least a foot away from the point my hand could reach. My hands were now fully stretched out, I tried my best to stretch it further. My face pressed against the metal of the barricade as I tried harder, but then I realized, the leaf was definitely not within my reach. Disappointed, I just gave up. Just when I was about to get up to leave the premises without the neem leaf, I felt something moving behind me. I turned around and saw an elderly lady applying the most innovative idea to help me get that one leaf. She had taken off her shawl to swipe it on the floor so that she could move the neem leaf towards me. Looking at her I realized that she was quite older than me. I watched her as she swirled her shawl on the floor that moved the leaf within my reach. I was still watching her when she asked me to pick up the leaf. Almost like a machine, I obeyed her. I leaned forward to pick up the leaf. It was now easily doable. I picked up it up and stood up. Happy to have got what I wanted, I turned back to thank the lady, who was standing right behind me. Or so I presumed, because when I turned around, the lady was gone.

There wasn't much of a crowd at that moment. So, I looked towards the front which could have been the way she had walked away. To my dismay I couldn't spot her anywhere. It must not have taken more than a few seconds to pick up the leaf and stand up. Where could she have disappeared in just few seconds? My eyes kept on searching for her, while I turned 360 degrees to spot her. But she was nowhere to be seen.

She was an elderly lady, yet she could bend down in a fraction of a second and swiftly swipe her shawl. Questions started playing in my head.

She bent down just to get me a leaf. Why, Sai?

She didn't wait to pick up a leaf for herself. Why, Sai?

In few seconds she could get out my sight. How, Sai?

She didn't speak anything more that the two words, "*Utha Lo*" (Pick up). Why, Sai?

Who was she, Sai?

Why did she help me, Sai?

Was that you, Sai?

Till this day, I don't understand what that moment was about. I couldn't even thank her. Let me leave it at that by saying "Sai and his ways are always miraculous".

14

THE MAGIC CONTINUES

I looked at my watch. It was past 6am. "Now I am really getting late", I said to myself. The driver was supposed to pick me up at 7am, I needed to rush back to the hotel. While still trying to wrap my head around the things that were happening since morning, I hurried towards the exit of the temple through the hallway.

The walk to the exit wasn't a short distance. By then, the number of people inside the temple had also reasonably increased. Some were headed towards the temple, some were just talking amongst themselves, a couple of elderly women, draped in saree in the traditional Marathi style, were sitting in the hallway. Two children were playing around them. I saw everything but noticed nothing. I was not running, but definitely rushing, with no intention to waste a moment more.

I was still inside the mandir premises. Mandir has many sales outlets which are owned by the trust. They sell few merchandises of Sai baba at a reasonable price. They are mostly inside the mandir, barring a few which are just outside the temple premises. The counters had opened up by then. I saw more people on my way out, walking, talking, shopping. Just on my way out, towards my left side I saw a shop inside the mandir premises. There was nothing exceptional about it, except that there were a few *chunris* (veils) on display outside this shop.

I was still inside the mandir premises. I walked past the shop as usual. But just a few steps ahead, I suddenly stopped to turn back to see what's there in that shop. It was such an involuntary action, given that I was already done with my darshan and had purchased whatever I had to, the previous night itself.

I peeped in to see lots of cloths there. Two guys were setting up the *chunris* (a piece of cloth to be offered to god) on the shelves. There were long shelves with 5-6 racks running across the walls of the shop, all with rods to hold the *chunris* on display. On the right side was the billing counter with a computer and a printer and a tray top to place the cloths selected by the devotees for billing. They were still setting up the shop and asked me to wait.

Both the guys were busy doing their job while I found an off-white plastic chair to sit on. I was not tired at all. In fact, after the beautiful morning and the amazing connect I felt with Baba, my energy level was as high as a football player dribbling the ball in a match. But I sat down, observing them as they did their job.

As I sat there, I started looking around to see what all I could buy. Red and pink were the colours that grabbed all my attention. It was nice to see such beautiful chunris, with so much of work done on them. I asked the guys who were still busy placing them on the shelves, "Bhaiya are these supposed to be given to baba for his *shringaar*?" He answered, "No. These are a prasaad of Baba".

I felt unsure of why I was there in the shop at all. I did not want to buy a *chunri* for myself, but then I thought of buying one for Riya. It was around 6.15am and I was already very late. The two guys were still busy in their work, setting up their shop systematically. From my chair, I looked around to finalize the one which I would eventually buy.

It took them about ten more minutes to finish setting up everything as per their liking. Once they were through, one guy picked up a broom and started dusting the floor and gently asked me to go out of the shop and wait. I was already late and understood that he was going to take some more time. Undecided whether to wait or to go back to the hotel, I moved out of the shop and stood at the door.

The scene outside the shop was still the same. People walked around, men, women, children, et al.

"Hope you had a Darshan?" a voice asked me.

It was a security guard, wearing the uniform of Shri Sai Baba Sansthan Trust. Funny that I didn't quite notice him coming up to me.

I replied with gratitude, "Oh yes, Bhaiya. Thrice!!".

He smiled and asked me to buy the cloth and then wait outside the shop for 5 minutes till he returned. I was undeniably late and the last thing I intended to do was WAIT.

Why did he ask me to wait?

I wondered a bit, but then again shifted my focus to the shop. Soon they finished the setup and I was called in. Along with me, quite a few more people entered the shop. I had intended to buy only one *chunri*, but ended up buying three of them. Beige, green and off-white were the colours, for three of my loved owns. I knew all three of them would be happy to have them. The chunris would be specially valued by them, I could tell, since I was taking them from Shirdi. I asked for a bag but they did not have any. It became quite a big bundle, piled one on top of the other. It was quite a task to carry them without even a string to tie them together. But I was happy to have purchased them, I didn't mind the trouble at all.

Once I came out of the shop, I remembered the security guard and his weird instruction. He had asked me to wait. I looked around but could not find anyone. I also realized that I couldn't remember his face much. I was in two minds, should I wait or leave for the hotel.

I had much stuff in my hand, I didn't look at my watch, but I could tell that it was way past the time I could afford to spend at the temple. One part of me was getting restless, I didn't feel the need to wait, especially after the beautiful darshan and connect I had at Dwarkamai. But another part of me was curious.

My curiosity got the better of me. I waited, more because of dilemma than decisiveness.

In few minutes, I heard a voice from the right side. "Bhaiya!"

I turned around to look at him. He was the same security guard. Strangely enough, this time too, I had not particularly seen him coming.

I kept staring at him while he offered me a few packets of UDI (the holy ash from the fire that Baba had lit) and a flower. He the sweetest voice, he said, "This is for you from Sai Baba. He has sent this for you from the mandir".

Almost on prompt, I opened my right hand to collect them. When he gently placed them on my hand, I touched them on my head.

It's one thing to be confused, it's another thing to be clueless. I think, I was more on the latter. I couldn't fathom why and how things were happening the way they were happening. I was trying to think so hard but my mind was absolutely blank.

I had forgotten all about the time and that I was getting late. However, I had begun walking towards the exit after putting the flower and UDI in my pocket. I was still holding the bundle of *chunris* in my hand.

I didn't quite notice him, but I could tell that the security guard was following me. I came out into the open area. The weather seemed pleasantly beautiful and complimented the greenery right in front at the Lendi Baugh. I looked back and saw him coming towards me.

Is he expecting some money?

It's a general practice in India by the Pandits to offer flowers and prasad to the devotees in Mandir and expect money in return. But he wasn't a pandit. He was just an ordinary security guy.

A few unanswered questions kept swaying through my mind.

Why did he ask me to wait?

Why did he go all the way inside the mandir?

Why did he bother to get the flower and prasad for me?

The reason my mind could come up with is that probably he wanted some money.

The thought crossed my mind as I stopped walking, waiting for him to reach me.

He walked up to me and pointed out at Nanda Deep, just near the Lendi Baugh. "Go there and take a Parikrama before you leave the temple premises", he said. It neither sounded like a request, nor an order, yet he sounded very intentional. I was still confused, wondering what was happening. I think he had read my mind as I kept looking at him. He asked me, "Where are you from and when are you returning back?"

"I am from Kolkata. I am returning back today only, in fact in a while from now", I replied.

Even as I spoke to him, I remembered how dangerously late I was getting. But I didn't hurry, still not sure, why!

At that instance, I recollected that it was the same guy who had led me to the counter to collect the Kakkar Aarti pass the previous night. I thanked him for his service and for the Udi and flower he had just brought me. I didn't pay him anything, in fact I had forgotten about any money when I looked at him. I spoke with a smile, genuinely thanking him for everything. His eyes just pointed towards the Nandadeep. I knew, he was insisting that I do the parikrama.

I did not know before that moment that Nandadeep existed there in Shirdi. I had never even noticed it before that day. I became curious to see, what was it like from close by. From a distance it looked like a very small, standalone mandir, barricaded just like any other important area of the temple. A short flight of stairs inside the barricade led to the entrance of mandir. On all the four sides there was some space to move around. I proceeded to the security guard's instructions.

Holding the heavy bundle of *chunris* with both my hands, somehow supporting the weight with my chest, I took three rounds of Nandadeep and came down. Once I completed the parikrama, I looked around, trying to look for the security guard. To my utter bewilderment, there wasn't another soul around. I was just alone there. I looked at a distance, there I saw that same security guy along with other guards talking amongst themselves. There was nothing more to say to him, so I moved out of the mandir, still engrossed in my thoughtlessness.

I crossed the road a bit carefully as I wasn't wearing slippers and got hold of an auto that dropped me to the hotel in just 2-3 minutes. I rushed up to the room. I had to get ready to leave.

That flower he had given me has now dried up, but I have preserved it in a pouch which is kept safely kept in my almirah.

15

BEGINNING, ALL OVER AGAIN

Once I was there in the room, I realized how much I was craving for my morning tea. I quickly had some biscuits and tea that didn't just quench my craving, but also helped me relax and think more carefully. It was past 7am already and the only thing that was playing in my mind was that the taxi guy would be waiting downstairs for me. I looked at the watch and mentally calculated all the things I was yet to do: Minimum 20 mins to shower up, get ready and pack up bags, 15 mins to checkout and pay the bill and another 15 mins to eat breakfast.

God, this is going to make the driver unhappy.

I like to adhere to my commitments, be it time or anything else. Not being able to keep my time commitment to the driver made me restless.

Unfortunately, I couldn't help it. I had a long day ahead and these were tasks that I couldn't possibly avoid. I did what I could do best at that time: HURRY.

I entered the bathroom to freshen up. As always, the mobile was on the table top. I went about my business when suddenly the mobile rang.

That must me mom.

I was expecting a call from my Mom anyway. I reached out for the mobile, almost certain that it was her call. But it was from an unknown number.

The moment I received the call, I heard a heavy and tired voice from the other end. "Hello, hello, aapka Puna drop hai na?". (Hello Sir. You have a drop to Pune. Right?) I guessed it was the driver. He definitely sounded worried.

"Yes", I said, "But via Shingnapur".

"Okay. I am coming in 10 mins".

Two thoughts flashed through my mind, almost simultaneously. First thought was, "Thank god, he has not yet arrived". The very next thought was, "It is impossible for me to be ready in 10 mins."

Even as the thoughts were playing in my head, I realized something which was evident from his voice: he sounded sleepy. I figured that he had just woken up.

Even before I could confirm this, he said, "*Neend nahi khula bhaiya* (I couldn't wake up brother). Sorry, I am late. I'll come in 10 mins". I replied, "No hurry, bhaiya. *Mere ko time hai abhi. Aap half an hour mein aajaiye* (I need more time, you come in half an hour)".

He hung up happily. I got thinking and smiled to myself, experiencing another little *leela* of Sai.

A minute back I thought of saying sorry to him and he said sorry instead over that call.

While I watched my daily series from the comfort of my home in Kolkata, I saw the *leelas* of Sai that he used to do to the people who had the good fortune of meeting Him. I wasn't aware that he was doing the same right there in front of me, inside me. *"How many times during this trip itself did I witness His magic?"*, I had lost count. It is impossible to put into words the feelings that I have been through, but still I hope that the readers of this book will be able to feel a bit of what I have lived in those moments. The joy of writing them is purely reliving those moments with goosebumps, smiles and happiness all over again. To top it all, the feel of his blessings seems like an icing on a cake.

It was a little past 8 when I finally got into the car and proceeded towards Shani Shingnapur. This was the first time ever in my life that I had planned to visit there.

It is a popular saying that until you visit Shingnapur, your trip to Shirdi is incomplete. But I had never had an urge or ever bothered to go there in any of my trips to Shirdi before. Thoughts aplenty crowded my head. I was feeling blessed and rewarded in every sense. My mind ran through the chain of events that I had been experiencing ever since I had left Kolkata.

This trip was no ordinary trip for me. Not only was I visiting Shirdi after a long time, it had taken me a few years of longing to get this opportunity. Memories of the past trips and miracles of this trip intertwined with each other, weaving a beautiful veil that covered my mind.

My life had gone through the lowest and toughest times during the last few years. I had often wondered, what kept me together? How did I even get through those times and reach this moment of success and glory?

No one could have imagined that I would emerge out of the rough tides in such a way.

"But here I am, mentally strong and emotionally resilient", I whispered to myself. It is this strength that gave me the power to recognize, how much more I had to contribute to others. I had realized long ago that had Sai not shown me the path, I would have never been so committed to contribute back to the society at large through my rehabilitation center.

Thanks to Sai, I have found my purpose.

The thought of the rehabilitation center made me smile. It was presently my dream project. My mind went back to listing what all I had to do for this dream project: the building had to be readied, the interiors had to be renovated, permissions had to be acquired, and most importantly, a name was yet to be selected...

I didn't realize when the car had crossed the town of Shirdi. It was speeding through the outskirts when all of a sudden, amidst all the thoughts rushing through my head, I heard a voice. I could instantly recall, it was the same voice I had heard at the mandir during Kakkar Aarti. It was the voice of MY Sai Baba.

He said a word.

Just One word.

SABHURI!

Why suddenly this word, Baba?

The next moment, it felt like a hundred bulbs were lit up in my head.

"SABHURI REHABILITATION CENTRE"

YESSSS! THAT'S THE NAME!

I had spent hours thinking about the perfect name for my dream project. A zillion words would come to my head, but nothing ever felt good enough.

And here I was, clearly visualizing the name, as if it was meant to be that only. My concern for months was solved within a few seconds by Baba. I could feel my heart beating faster than ever before, so overwhelmed I was.

"Sai, Sai, Sai, Mere Sai... you know what is good for me, what is meant for me and what to give me when its suitable for me. Your ways are miraculous and your protection is a shield for your children. Your love is unconditional and your blessings invaluable. The biggest gift you have given me today is the feeling that in each moment of my life, I have your love and I am grateful for it. Your miracles have not only changed, but given a new meaning to my life. I have found a new way to understand myself. The confidence and the strength that you give me to take instant decisions: they are nothing but your blessings. Whatever I am, wherever I am today, it's all with your blessings. I know that my life is still incomplete but my trust and belief in you are unshakable. They always remind me that I shall get only what you have decided for me and whenever it is destined for me. You have two weapons, which are always there with me and they keep reminding me of the days when I stopped trusting you, something that I wouldn't dare to do again. They are nothing but the most two beautiful words...

SHRADDHA AND SABHURI

(Faith and Patience)

I spoke almost in one breath, but I HAD to thank my Sai Baba.

Every time I have been through crisis or questions, I have always found the answers in my Sai, in those two magical words:

These were the only two things that have kept me going in my darkest hours. My SHRADDHA in my Sai Baba and my SABHURI kept reminding me that my Sai is there with me. I have often told this sentence to many people in my life, *"Jab wo din nahi rahe to ye din bhi nahi rehenge"*

(When those days didn't stay then these too shall pass). Shraddha and Sabhuri can take you through the toughest times.

This trip was just another proof how his *leela* works in my life. At every step, He gave proof of His presence, guiding me, blessing me, showing me that His divine power truly rules me life.

I couldn't stop smiling as I felt his Divine grace and presence in my life. I don't know if the driver had seen me smiling to myself though his rear-view mirror. Honestly, I didn't even care. I was too busy in my conversation with My Sai.

"You won't stop amazing me, will you Baba?", I asked Him.

He smiled.

I saw Him.

MIRACLES OF SAI WITH SUJAY KHANDELWAL

Miracles of Sai with Sujay Khandelwal is a channel on YouTube with it's pages on Facebook & Instagram. It was Sainath's wish himself that these media platforms be created & reach out to the devotees across the universe.

Miracles are Out of the box extraordinary pleasant happening in our lives by **Divine Almighty.** The **Manganous Omnipresent** Sai Baba a blessing to mankind comes to rescue of anyone who earnestly asks for help and bails him out of trouble which has happened with millions of people over decades.

This channel endeavours to bring to you first-hand experience of such Miracles by the recipient themselves so that you can relate to them easily and benefit out of it.

By the grace of Sai Samarth many people have benefited immensely and over the decades and now over a century such Miracles keep happening in lives of people across the globe.

Go ahead try and connect to Baba and feel the divine experiences which can really change your life.

Om Sairam 🙏

SABHURI RAHABILITATION CENTRE

Sabhuri Rehabilitation Centre is loving nest for those who are seeking to get out of clutches of a disease called Addiction (Drugs and Alcoholism).

It's a wing of an NGO **Shiv Chandra Charitable Trust** founded by the **Khandelwal family** for the welfare of the society.

Sabhuri aims to provide support to those who are engulfed with the menace of this dreadful disease which ruins self and their loved ones.

We aim to cure them with utmost love and creating a congenial environment around them so that they can recover and get back to Life.

It was Sainath's wish that this organisation be formed to help to society to fight against the **3rd most fatal disease in the world-ADDICTION** which is highly ignored by the society.

Address :- Sabhuri Rehabilitation Centre
Block – CB 28, Salt lake Sector – 1,
Kolkata – 700064, West Bengal
Contact :- +91 6289392832
website :- www.sabhuri.in

SHIKSHAYAAN

The idea of - empowering our help - House help, drivers, office Peon, Labours, to overcome low literacy problem is brainchild of Mr Sujay Khandelwal, Trustee of SHIV CHANDRA CHARITABLE TRUST.

A personal initiative, resulting in – **SHIKSHA YAAN - the Adult Literacy Programme.**

Sujay appeals to you to join this mission by committing 72 hours of your life. Contribute, at least 15 minutes a day to provide the basic literacy to people with whom we interact in our daily life.

This can accelerate the spread of literacy in India

website :- www.shikshayaan.in

Books on
SHIRDI SAI BABA

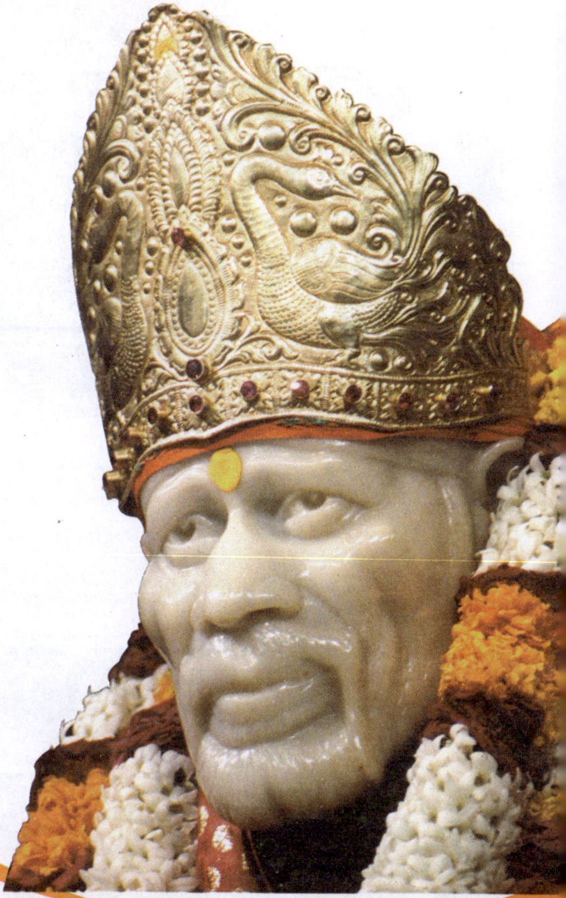

STERLING

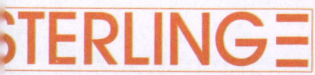

NEW BOOKS

2020-2021

New Findings on Shridi Sai Baba
CHANDRABHANU SATPATHY
978 93 86245 52 6
5.5"×8.5"
222pp
Paperback ₹ 300

शिरडी साईं बाबा नवीन तथ्य
चन्द्रभानु सतपथी
978 93 86245 63 2
5.5"×8.5"
224pp
Paperback ₹ 300

COFFEE TABLE BOOK

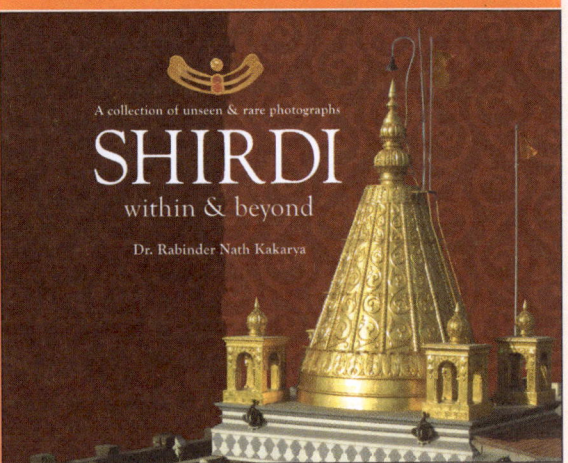

Shirdi Sai Baba is a household name in India as well as in many parts of the World today. Sterling Publishers are well known for publishing the largest number of books on Shirdi Sai, indeed far more than any other publisher. We endeavour to be comprehensive in the range of author and content. We also publish books on other saints and masters.

SHIRDI : within & beyond
A collection of unseen & rare photographs
Dr. Rabinder Nath Kakarya
978 81 207 7806 1   ₹ 750

शिरडी अंतः से अनंत
डॉ. रबिन्द्रनाथ ककरिया
978 81 207 8191 7
₹ 750

STERLING   mail@sterlingpublishers.in

NEW **NEW** **NEW**

Shri Sai Satcharita
The Life and Teachings of
Shirdi Sai Baba
Translated by Indira Kher
ISBN 978 81 207 2211 8
₹ 600(HB)
ISBN 978 81 207 2153 1
₹ 500(PB)

**Shri Shirdi Saibaba Gems
From His Philosophical
Teachings**
ISBN 978 81 944007 3 8
₹ 300

**Prema Rathna
Radhakrishnayaee**
ISBN 978 81 947772 0 5
₹ 100

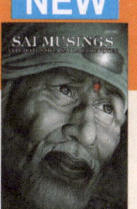

Sai Musings
ISBN 978 81 950824 5 2
₹ 300

**Shirdi Sai Baba: The
Universal Master**
Sri Kaleshwar
ISBN 978 81 207 9664 5
₹ 150

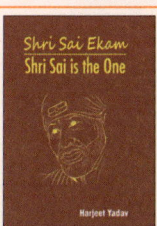

**Shri Sai Ekam
Shri Sai is the One**
Harjeet Yadav
978 93 86245 38 0
₹ 900

**Shri Sai Baba
Teachings & Philosophy**
Lt Col M B Nimbalkar
ISBN 978 81 207 2364 1
₹ 150

Shirdi Sai Baba
Anusuya Vasudevan
ISBN 978 93 86245 16 8
(64 pages plates)
₹ 200

**We need Sai forever... at 6,
16 and 60!**
Saurabh Khanna
ISBN 978 93 86245 15 1
₹ 190

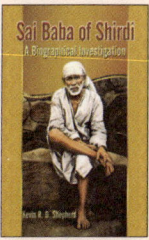

**Sai Baba of Shirdi:
A Biographical Investigation**
Kevin R. D. Shepherd
ISBN 978 81 207 9901 1
₹ 450

**The Eternal Sai
Consciousness**
A. R. Nanda
ISBN 978 81 207 9043 8
₹ 200

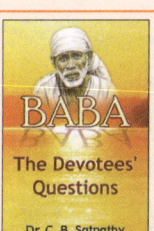

**BABA:
The Devotees' Questions**
Dr. C. B. Satpathy
ISBN 978 81 207 8966 1
₹ 150

**The Loving God:
Story of Shirdi Sai Baba**
Dr. G. R. Vijayakumar
ISBN 978 81 207 8079 8
₹ 200

**Sai Samartha and Ramana
Maharshi**
S. Seshadri
ISBN 978 81 207 8986 9
₹ 150

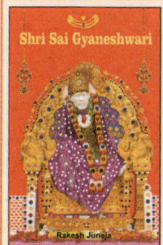

Shri Sai Gyaneshwari
Rakesh Juneja
ISBN 978 93 86245 05 2
₹ 300

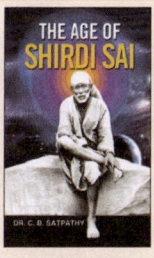

The Age of Shirdi Sai
Dr. C. B. Satpathy
ISBN 978 81 207 8700 1
₹ 300

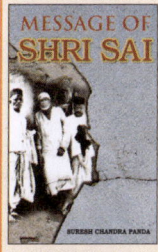

Message of Shri Sai
Suresh Chandra Panda
ISBN 978 81 207 9512 9
₹ 150

A Divine Journey with Baba
Vinny Chitluri
ISBN 978 81 207 9859 5
₹ 300

Sai Baba: Faqir of Shirdi
Kevin R.D. Shepherd
ISBN 978 93 86245 06 9
₹ 350

mail@sterlingpublishers.in

STERLING

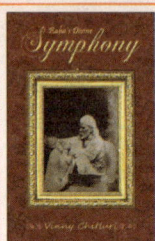
Baba's Divine Symphony
Vinny Chitluri
ISBN 978 81 207 8485 7
₹ 300

Sai Baba an Incarnation
Bela Sharma
ISBN 978 81 207 8833 6
₹ 200

Shirdi Sai Baba: The Perfect Master
Suresh Chandra Panda & Smita Panda
ISBN 978 81 207 8113 9
₹ 200

The Eternal Sai Phenomenon
A R Nanda
ISBN 978 81 207 6086 8
₹ 200

Baba's Rinanubandh
Leelas during His Sojourn in Shirdi
Compiled by Vinny Chitluri
ISBN 978 81 207 3403 6
₹ 300

Baba's Gurukul SHIRDI
Vinny Chitluri
ISBN 978 81 207 4770 8
₹ 250

Baba's Anurag
Love for His Devotees
Compiled by Vinny Chitluri
ISBN 978 81 207 5447 8
₹ 200

Baba's Vaani: His Sayings and Teachings
Compiled by Vinny Chitluri
ISBN 978 81 207 3859 1
₹ 250

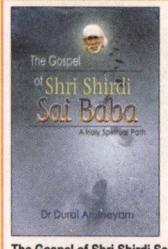
The Gospel of Shri Shirdi Sai Baba: A Holy Spiritual Path
Dr Durai Arulneyam
ISBN 978 81 207 3997 0
₹ 150

Jagat Guru: Shri Shirdi Sai Baba
Prasada Jagannadha Rao
ISBN 978 81 207 8175 7
₹ 100

Spotlight on the Sai Story
Chakor Ajgaonker
ISBN 978 81 207 4399 1
₹ 200

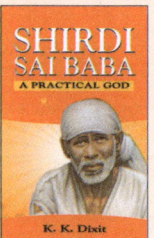
Shirdi Sai Baba A Practical God
K. K. Dixit
ISBN 978 81 207 5918 3
₹ 75

Promises of Shirdi Sai Baba (The Eleven Precious Sayings)
Bela Sharma
ISBN 978 93 85913 98 3
₹ 75

Shirdi Sai Baba The Divine Healer
Raj Chopra
ISBN 978 81 207 4766 1
₹ 150

Shirdi Sai Baba and other Perfect Masters
C B Satpathy
ISBN 978 81 207 2384 9
₹ 200

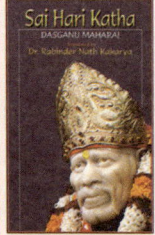
Sai Hari Katha
Dasganu Maharaj
Translated by
Dr. Rabinder Nath Kakarya
ISBN 978 81 207 3324 4
₹ 150

Unravelling the Enigma: Shirdi Sai Baba in the light of Sufism
Marianne Warren
ISBN 978 81 207 2147 0
₹ 400

I am always with you
Lorraine Walshe-Ryan
ISBN 978 81 207 3192 9
₹ 150

BABA- May I Answer
C.B. Satpathy
ISBN 978 81 207 4594 0
₹ 150

Ek An English Musical on the Life of Shirdi Sai Baba
Usha Akella
ISBN 978 81 207 6842 0
₹ 75

STERLING mail@sterlingpublishers.in

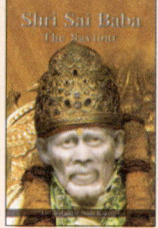

Sri Sai Baba
Sai Sharan Anand
Translated by V.B Kher
ISBN 978 81 207 1950 7
₹ 200

Sai Baba: His Divine Glimpses
V B Kher
ISBN 978 81 207 2291 0
₹ 95

A Diamond Necklace To: Shirdi Sai Baba
Giridhar Ari
ISBN 978 81 207 5868 1
₹ 200

Life History of Shirdi Sai Baba
Ammula Sambasiva Rao
ISBN 978 81 207 7722 4
₹ 250

Shri Sai Baba- The Saviour
Dr. Rabinder Nath Kakarya
ISBN 978 81 207 4701 2
₹ 100

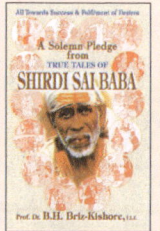

Sai Baba's 261 Leelas
Balkrishna Panday
ISBN 978 81 207 2727 4
₹ 200

A Solemn Pledge from True Tales of Shirdi Sai Baba
Dr B H Briz-Kishore
ISBN 978 81 207 2240 8
₹ 95

God Who Walked on Earth: The Life & Times of Shirdi Sai Baba
Rangaswami Parthasarathy
ISBN 978 81 207 1809 8
₹ 225

Shri Shirdi Sai Baba: His Life and Miracles
ISBN 978 81 207 2877 6
₹ 35

Shirdi Sai Baba Aratis
ISBN 978 81 207 8456 7
(English)
₹ 10

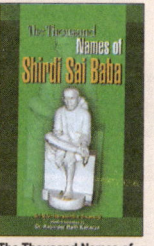
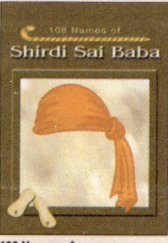

Sree Sai Charitra Darshan
Mohan Jagannath Yadav
ISBN 978 81 207 8346 1
₹ 225

The Miracles of Sai Baba
ISBN 978 81 207 5433 1 (HB)
₹ 300

The Thousand Names of Shirdi Sai Baba
Sri B.V. Narasimha Swami Ji
Hindi translation by
Dr. Rabinder Nath Kakarya
ISBN 978 81 207 3738 9
₹ 75

108 Names of Shirdi Sai Baba
ISBN 978 81 207 3074 8
₹ 50

Shirdi Sai Speaks... Sab Ka Malik Ek
Quotes for the Day
ISBN 978 81 207 3101 1
₹ 200

DIVINE GURUS

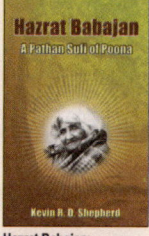

Guru Charitra
Shree Swami Samarth
ISBN 978 81 207 3348 0
₹ 300

Sri Swami Samarth Maharaj of Akkalkot
N.S. Karandikar
ISBN 978 81 207 3445 6
₹ 250

Hazrat Babajan: A Pathan Sufi of Poona
Kevin R. D. Shepherd
ISBN 978 81 207 8698 1
₹ 200

Sri Narasimha Swami Apostle of Shirdi Sai Baba
Dr. G.R. Vijayakumar
ISBN 978 81 207 4432 5
₹ 90

Lord Sri Dattatreya The Trinity
Dwarika Mohan Mishra
ISBN 978 81 207 5417 1
₹ 200

mail@sterlingpublishers.in

STERLING

श्री साई सच्चरित्र
श्री शिरडी साई बाबा की अद्भुत जीवनी तथा उनके अमूल्य उपदेश
गोविंद रघुनाथ दाभोलकर (हेमाडपंत)
978 81 207 2500 3
₹ 400 (HB)

श्री साई ज्ञानेश्वरी- महाकाव्य
राकेश जुनेजा
978 93 86245 17 5
₹ 250

हमें साई की आवश्यकता है सदा के लिए 6, 16 और 60!
सौरभ खत्रा
978 93 86245 21 2
₹ 125

साई ही क्यों?
राकेश जुनेजा
978 81 207 9610 2
₹ 200

जेल में साई साक्षात्कार
राकेश जुनेजा
978 81 207 9507 5
₹ 150

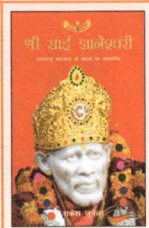
श्री साई ज्ञानेश्वरी
राकेश जुनेजा
978 81 207 9491 7
₹ 250

शिडी साई बाबा के ग्यारह अनमोल वचन
बेला शर्मा
978 93 85913 97 6
₹ 75

श्री साई चरित्र दर्शन
मोहन जगन्नाथ यादव
978 81 207 8350 8
₹ 200

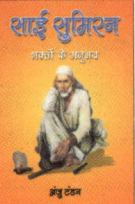
साई सुमिरन
अंजु टंडन
978 81 207 8706 3
₹ 100

बाबा की वाणी-उनके वचन तथा आदेश
बेला शर्मा
978 81 207 4745 6
₹ 100

बाबा का अनुराग
विनी चितलुरी
978 81 207 6699 0
₹ 125

बाबा का ऋणानुबंध
विनी चितलुरी
978 81 207 5998 5
₹ 150

बाबा का गुरूकुल-शिरडी
विनी चितलुरी
978 81 207 6698 3
₹ 150

बाबा-आध्यात्मिक विचार
चन्द्रभानु सतपथी
978 81 207 4627 5
₹ 175

पृथ्वी पर अवतरित भगवान शिरडी के साई बाबा
रंगास्वामी पार्थसारथी
978 81 207 2101 2
₹ 200

साई बाबा एक अवतार
बेला शर्मा
978 81 207 6706 5
₹ 150

साई सत् चरित का प्रकाश
बेला शर्मा
978 81 207 7804 7
₹ 200

श्री शिरडी साई बाबा एवं अन्य सद्गुरु
चन्द्रभानु सतपथी
978 81 207 4401 1
₹ 90

साई शरण में
चन्द्रभानु सतपथी
978 81 207 2802 8
₹ 150

साई - सबका मालिक
कल्पना शाकुनी
978 81 207 9886 1
₹ 200

श्री साई बाबा के परम भक्त
डॉ. रविन्द्रनाथ ककरिया
978 81 207 2779 3
₹ 125

शिरडी अंतः से अनंत
डॉ. रविन्द्रनाथ ककरिया
978 81 207 8191 7
₹ 750

STERLING mail@sterlingpublishers.in

श्री साईं बाबा के अनन्य भक्त
डॉ. रविन्द्र नाथ ककरिया
978 81 207 2705 2
₹ 100

साई का संदेश
डॉ. रविन्द्र नाथ ककरिया
978 81 207 2879 0
₹ 200

श्री साईं बाबा के उपदेश व तत्वज्ञान
लेफ्टिनेन्ट कर्नल एम. बी. निंबालकर
978 81 207 5971 8
₹ 100

साई भक्तानुभव
डॉ. रविन्द्रनाथ ककरिया
978 81 207 3052 6
₹ 125.

मुक्तिदाता - श्री साईं बाबा
डॉ. रविन्द्रनाथ ककरिया
978 81 207 2778 6
₹ 65

साईं दत्तावधूता
राजेन्द्र भण्डारी
978 81 207 4400 4
₹ 75

साईं हरि कथा
दासगणु महाराज
978 81 207 3323 7
₹ 65

श्री नरसिम्हा स्वामी शिरडी साईं बाबा के दिव्य प्रचारक
डॉ. रविन्द्र नाथ ककरिया
978 81 207 4437 0
₹ 100

शिरडी साईं बाबा - की सत्य कथाओं से प्राप्त - एक पावन प्रतिज्ञा
प्रो. डॉ. बी.एच. ब्रिज-किशोर
978 81 207 2346 7
₹ 95

दिव्य भजन
डॉ. रविन्द्रनाथ ककरिया
978 81 207 9505 1
₹ 125

शिरडी संपूर्ण दर्शन
डॉ. रविन्द्रनाथ ककरिया
978 81 207 2312 2
₹ 50

शिरडी साईं बाबा की दिव्य लीलाएँ
डॉ. रविन्द्र नाथ ककरिया
978 81 207 6376 0
₹ 150

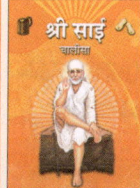
श्री साईं चालीसा
978 81 207 4773 9
₹ 50

शिरडी साईं बाबा आरती
978 81 207 8195 5
₹ 10

आरती संग्रह
(3D cover)
on Plastic
ISBN 978 81 207 8940 1
Size: 14.20 x 10.70 cm
₹ 60

आरती संग्रह
(Index Boardbook)
Gold/Silver Cover
ISBN 978 81 207 9057 5
Size: 10.70 x 15.45 cm
₹ 100

आरती संग्रह
(Boardbook)
Green Cover
ISBN 978 81 207 4774 6
Size: 11 x 15 cm
(9 Leafs)
₹ 50

शिरडी साई के दिव्य वचन-सब का मालिक एक प्रतिदिन का विचार
978 81 207 3533 0
₹ 200

ORIYA LANGUAGE

ଶ୍ରୀ ସାଇ ପ୍ରକଟିତ
(Oriya)
978 81 207 8332 4
₹ 350

ସାଇ ସନ୍ଦେଶ
978 81 207 9534 1
₹ 100

ଶ୍ରୀ ଶିରିଡ଼ି ସାଇବାବାଙ୍କ କଥାମୃତ
ପ୍ରଫେସର୍ ଡ. ବି. ଏଚ. ବ୍ରିଜକିଶୋର
978 81 207 7774 3
₹ 95

ଶ୍ରୀ ସାଇବାବାଙ୍କ
978 81 207 9982 0
₹ 125

ଶିରିଡ଼ି ସାଇ ବାବାଙ୍କ ଜୀବନ ଚରିତ (Oriya)
978 81 207 7417 9
₹ 125

mail@sterlingpublishers.in

STERLING

KANNAD LANGUAGE

Shirdi Sai Baba Aratis (Kannada)
₹ 10

ಬಾಬಾರವರ ಯುಗಾನುಬಂಧ
ಬ್ರಿಜ್-ಕಿಶೋರ್
978 81 207 9500 6
₹ 200

(Kannada)
ಪ್ರೊ. ಡಾ. ಬಿ.ಎಚ್.
ಬ್ರಿಜ್-ಕಿಶೋರ್
978 81 207 2873 8
₹ 95

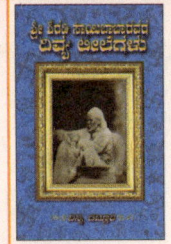
978 81 207 8930 2
₹ 225

ಪಯಣ
ಬ್ರಿಜ್ ಕಿಶೋರ್
978 81 207 9975 2
₹ 200

TAMIL AND TELUGU LANGUAGE

MARATHI LANGUAGE

NEW

Life History of Sri Shirdi Sai Baba
978-93-86245-77-9
₹ 250

(Tamil)
ಪ್ರೊ. ಡಾ. ಬಿ.ಎಚ್. ಬ್ರಿಜ್-ಕಿಶೋರ್
978 81 207 2876 9 ₹ 95

Shirdi Sai Baba Aratis
(Telugu) ₹ 10
(Tamil) ₹ 10

ಷಿರಡಿಸಾಯಿಬಾಬಾ
(Telugu)
ಪ್ರೊ. ಡಾ. ಬಿ.ಎಚ್. ಬ್ರಿಜ್-ಕಿಶೋರ್
978 81 207 2294 1 ₹ 95

शिर्डी साईबाबांची दिव्य वचने (Marathi) सबका मालिक एक दैनंदिन विचार
978 81 207 7518 3
₹ 200

THE THOUSAND NAMES OF GOD

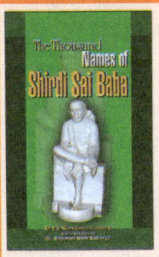
Shirdi Sai Baba
DR. RABINDER NATH KAKARYA
978 81 207 3738 9   ₹75

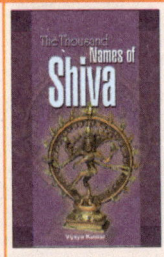
Shiva
VIJAYA KUMAR
978 81 207 3008 3   ₹75

Ganesha
VIJAYA KUMAR
978 81 207 3007 6   ₹75

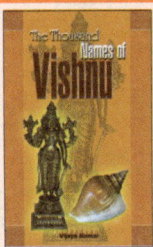
Vishnu
VIJAYA KUMAR
978 81 207 3009 0   ₹75

Colouring My Way
STERLING STUDIO
978 81 207 9790 1   ₹50

108 NAMES OF GOD

Lakshmi
978 81 207 2028 2   ₹50

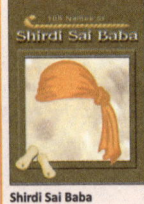
Shirdi Sai Baba
978 81 207 3074 8   ₹50

Durga
978 81 207 2027 5   ₹50

Shiva
978 81 207 2025 1   ₹50

Hanuman
978 81 207 2024 4   ₹50

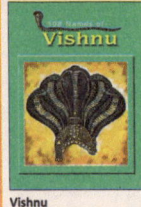
Vishnu
978 81 207 2023 7   ₹50

Sterling Publishers Private Limited
Plot No-13, Eco Tech-III, Udyog Kendra Greater Noida, Uttar Pradesh, Pin-201308 India
CIN: U22110DL1964PTC211907 GST: 09AAACS0306C1Z1
Phone No : +91 82877 98380   E-mail : mail@sterlingpublishers.in   www.sterlingpublishers.in
Prices are subject to change